Friendsight:

What Friends Know that Others Don't

Professional Papers

Bella DePaulo, Ph.D.

2011

CONTENTS

Preface

If you asked me about my professional interests, I would say that I studied the psychology of deceiving and detecting deceit for more than two decades, then focused my attention on an entirely different topic – the study of single people, and their place in society and in science. In so doing, I became more and more aware of the importance of friendship in the lives of many single people – and many other people, too.

So I set out to take a closer look at the psychology of friendship. That's when I realized that the topic of friendship has had an important place in my research as far back as 1980, which was just one year after I earned my Ph.D. from Harvard.

In *Friendsight: What Friends Know that Others Don't*, I have collected the five journal articles I co-authored in which friendship was featured most prominently. The articles were published over a span of nearly a quarter-century, yet discernible themes run though them all. For example: Do pairs of friends interpret their interpersonal worlds more similarly than do pairs of strangers? What do friends know that other people do not know? What do they seem not to want to know? Are friends more honest with each other than they are with strangers?

The five papers included in this book were all published originally in academic journals. That means that they are at times plagued with jargon and dotted with arcane statistics. Still, even the academically uninitiated should be able to make sense of the introductions and discussion sections of each article, and maybe even glean the key points from other parts as well.

I thank all of the co-authors who have contributed to these publications, and to the publishers for their permission to reprint the articles. I am also ever so grateful to all of the people who have asked me what I have learned about friendship in my research endeavors. These five papers are a big part of the answer to that question.

You can learn more about all of my research at my website, www.BellaDePaulo.com. My blog, *All Things Single (and More)* is at that site, as is information about all of my books. I also write the "Living Single" blog for *Psychology Today*. I love to hear from readers so feel free to get in touch.

Bella DePaulo
Summerland, California
March 2011

Journal of Nonverbal Behavior, 1980, *5*, 64-68

Similarities between Friends in their Understanding of Nonverbal Cues

Dorothea V. Brauer
Bella M. DePaulo

Friends are believed to be more similar to each other than are strangers along a variety of dimensions. In previous research, interest has focused on such variables as demographic characteristics, intelligence, personality, attitudes, and values (see Berscheid & Walster, 1978, for a review). Resemblances in attitudes and values suggest that friends see the world more similarly than people who are not friends. In this study we have examined similarities between friends (and strangers) in their interpretations of aspects of the social world – more specifically, in their reading of nonverbal cues. Since socioemotional considerations are likely to be extremely important in the development and maintenance of friendships (perhaps especially for women), congruences in social skill (e.g., skill in understanding emotional cues) may be powerful predictors of friendship status.

Many interpretations have been proposed to explain similarities between friends in attitudes and values. Two of the most common explanations are: (1) that friends select each other as friends on the basis of their initial similarities in attitudes and values, and (2) friends influence each other over the course of the relationship in such a way that they come to resemble each other more and more along these dimensions. Suggestive evidence for the latter interpretation would come from findings showing that long-term friends are more similar to each other than newly established friends. Of course, the two explanations are not mutually exclusive: friends might select each other on the basis of initial resemblances, and then become even more similar as their relationship develops. In this study, we have compared resemblances in nonverbal decoding skill between friends to resemblances between nonfriends; then, within the pairs of friends, we related the degree of similarity in their nonverbal judgments to aspects of their relationships, such as the length of their friendship and the intimacy of the topics that they discuss with each other.

METHOD

Subjects were 20 female undergraduates (10 pairs of friends) who volunteered to participate in a study of interpersonal sensitivity. Each subject independently completed a standardized test of nonverbal decoding ability and a questionnaire assessing aspects of the subject's relationship with her friend.

The nonverbal decoding task was the Still Photo version of the Profile of Nonverbal Sensitivity, or PONS test (Rosenthal, Hall, DiMatteo, Rogers, & Archer, 1979). The test consisted of 20

5

photographs of the face and 20 photographs of the body of a woman portraying a number of different everyday life situations (e.g., talking to a lost child, expressing gratitude, threatening someone, asking forgiveness). Subjects' task was to choose the appropriate label to describe each photograph from a pair of situation labels, only one of which correctly described the situation that the sender was portraying. Accuracy at understanding facial cues (face accuracy) was defined as the number of correct responses to the face photographs, while body accuracy was defined as the number of correct responses to the body photographs.

The friendship questionnaire listed 18 topics of conversation (e.g., classes, music, grades, dating, personal crises, personal inhibitions) which were classified by five judges as either casual, moderate, or intimate. The effective interrater reliability (Spearman-Brown) for this classification was .93. Each subject also indicated how long she had known her friend (responses were later assigned a value from 1 to 9; 1 = less than a year, 2 = one to two years, 3 = two to three years…9 = more than 8 years) and how much time (hours per week) she currently spends with this friend.

RESULTS

Intraclass correlations were computed for face and body accuracy to assess the degree of similarity between friends in their judgments of nonverbal cues. Intraclass correlations were originally developed in part to measure family resemblance (Snedecor & Cochran, 1967). A correlation of 1.00 was obtained when scores within dyads were identical (e.g., when both friends earn the same score) but scores from different dyads were not the same. An intraclass correlation of .00 was obtained when the variation of members of the same dyad (mean square within dyad) was equal to the variation of members of different dyads (mean square between dyads). Thus, when there was no real similarity in skills for friends, compared to people who are not friends, the expected value of the intraclass correlation was zero.

Friends showed a striking degree of similarity in their understanding of facial cues (intraclass r = .64, p = .01), but displayed a negligible degree of similarity in their decoding of body cues (r = .09, n.s.).

The next set of analyses focused only on similarities within pairs of friends. The degree of similarity within each pair was correlated with other aspects of the friendship assessed by the friendship questionnaire. Face similarity within each pair was indexed by the absolute difference in face accuracy scores between the two friends (smaller differences, of course, indicate greater similarity). Body similarity was computed analogously.

Each pair of friends was also assigned scores indicating the degree to which the friends discussed casual, moderate, and intimate topics. Casual scores were calculated by averaging, across the two friends, the number of casual topics they reported discussing with each other. Moderate and intimate scores were computed in the same way. Similarly, the length of the relationship and the amount of time spent together were defined as the mean of two friends' responses to these items.

Table 1 illustrates what the correlations were between the similarity scores and the relationship measures. Pairs of friends who were more similar in their understanding of facial cues (compared to those who were less similar) discussed a significantly greater number of different topics with each other. The relationship between face similarity and the intimacy of the topics discussed was especially noteworthy. This relationship – between the degree of similarity in facial decoding skill and number of topics discussed – was significant only for the intimate topics, and decreased monotonically from intimate to moderate to casual. Friends who were more similar to each other in their understanding of facial cues tended to be friends who had known each other longer, but who currently spent somewhat less time with each other than friends who were less similar to each other in face accuracy. (However, neither of these correlations was statistically significant.) Body accuracy was not significantly related to any of the friendship variables.

Table 1

The Relationship between Similarity in Nonverbal Decoding Skill
and Characteristics of the Friendship

	Similarity Scores	
Friendship Variables	*Face Accuracy*	*Body Accuracy*
Intimacy of Conversational Topics		
Intimate	-.71*	-.06
Moderate	-.41	.04
Casual	.13	.00
Total Number of Topics (Intimate + Moderate + Casual)	-.65*	-.02
Length of Friendship	-.49	-.21
Amount of Time Spent Together	.48	-.31

Note: Similarity scores are absolute difference scores. Thus, lower values indicate greater similarity.

*p < .05, two-tailed

DISCUSSION

In the present study, friends were more similar to each other in their understanding of facial cues of emotion than were people who were not friends. Friends were not more similar than strangers in their interpretations of body cues. Analyses of the friendship pairs further indicated that friends who were especially similar to each other in their ability to decode facial cues discussed a greater number of different topics with each other – especially intimate topics, had been friends for a longer period of time, but currently spent less time with each other than did friends who were less similar in face accuracy.

That skill congruence was differentially predicted by the length of the relationship and the intimacy of conversational topics, compared to the amount of time currently spent together, was consistent with the findings reported by Wheeler and Nezlek (1977) in their study of the social participation patterns of male and female undergraduates. Over a two-semester period, females, as compared to males, spent less time interacting with their three closest same-sex friends, but felt more satisfied with the quality of their relationships with those friends. For females, then, increases in the longevity of a relationship appeared to be associated with a decrease in the amount of time spent together but an increase in the satisfaction with the quality of the relationships.

The similarities that friends show in their judgments of facial cues can be explained in a number of ways. First, it might be hypothesized that people who are more similar to each other in the ways that they interpret their social world are more likely to select each other as friends, perhaps because of the fulfillment of the consensual validation that they could provide for each other. While this may be an important factor, our results suggest that friends' interactions with each other over the course of their relationship might also serve to increase the similarities between them in their understanding of facial cues.

First, friends who have been together for a longer period of time tend to be (nonsignficantly) more similar to each other in facial decoding. They also discuss a greater diversity of topics – especially intimate topics – with each other. Perhaps, friends who have been friends for a long time are especially likely to discuss and compare their interpretations of their social worlds. These discussions could have the effect of increasing the congruence in their interpretations of social signals, including nonverbal cues. Facial cues are likely to be more important than body cues in this regard because they are imbued with all sorts of social and personal significance (e.g., people believe that the eyes reveal a person's true character) (e.g., Argyle & Cook, 1976), because people are held more accountable for their facial cues than for their body cues (Ekman & Friesen, 1969), and because observers seem to be more attentive to the face than to the body when decoding nonverbal cues (cf. DePaulo, Rosenthal, Eisenstat, Rogers, & Finkelstein, 1978); DiMatteo & Hall, 1979).

Similarities between friends in their nonverbal decoding skills might also be a function of the similarities in their social worlds (cf. Blanck, Zuckerman, DePaulo & Rosenthal, in press). Two people who are friends, compared to two people who do not know each other, are more likely to be embedded in social networks that are comparable in the degree to which they encourage or discourage the development of skills such as interpersonal sensitivity. Finally, friends may also be more comparable than people who are not friends in the amount of practice that they have at decoding nonverbal cues and in the kinds of nonverbal cues that they tend to encounter in their everyday lives. Thus, friends may not only be more similar to strangers in how they see their social worlds; they may have more similar social worlds to see.

REFERENCES

Argyle, M., & Cook, M. *Gaze and mutual gaze*. Cambridge: Cambridge University Press, 1976.

Berscheid, E., & Walster, E. H. *Interpersonal attraction* (2nd ed.). Reading, MA: Addison-Wesley, 1978.

Blanck, P. D., Zuckerman, M., DePaulo, B. M., & Rosenthal, R. Sibling resemblances in nonverbal style and skill. *Journal of Nonverbal Behavior*, in press.

DePaulo, B. M., Rosenthal, R., Eisenstat, R. A., Rogers, P. L., & Finkelstein, S. Decoding discrepant nonverbal cues. *Journal of Personality and Social Psychology*, 1978, *36*, 313-323.

DiMatteo, M. R., & Hall, J. A. Nonverbal decoding skill and attention to nonverbal cues: A research note. *Environmental Psychology and Nonverbal Behavior*, 1979, *3*, 188-192.

Ekman, P., & Friesen, W. V. Nonverbal leakage and clues to deception. *Psychiatry*, 1969, *32*, 88-106.

Rosenthal, R., Hall, J. A., DiMatteo, M. R., Rogers, P. L., & Archer, D. *Sensitivity to nonverbal cues: The PONS test*. Baltimore: The Johns Hopkins University Press, 1979.

Snedecor, G. W., & Cochran, W. G. *Statistical methods*. Ames, Iowa: The Iowa State University Press, 1967.

Wheeler, L., & Nezlek, J. Sex differences in social participation. *Journal of Personality and Social Psychology*, 1977, *35*, 742-754.

Journal of Nonverbal Behavior, 1995, *19*, 135-149.

Familiarity Effects in Nonverbal Understanding:
Recognizing Our Own Facial Expressions and Our Friends'

Matthew E. Ansfield, Bella M. DePaulo, and Kathy L. Bell

In this study we explored how individuals' private expressions are interpreted by the self, same-sex friends, and strangers. Videotapes were made of participants as they watched pleasant, unpleasant, and unusual slides. Approximately a year later, the tapes were shown to the participant, a same-sex friend, another participant, and the other participant's friend. Judge were able to read the facial expressions at levels of accuracy that were significantly greater than chance. They were no better at reading familiar targets (themselves or their friends) than unfamiliar ones (strangers), with only one exception (men were better at recognizing the reactions of familiar targets than unfamiliar targets viewing pleasant slides). In their abilities to understand nonverbal cues, female friends showed resemblances to each other on all accuracy measures (pleasant/unpleasant/unusual x familiar/unfamiliar). Male friends resembled each other only in their understanding of the reactions of unfamiliar men viewing unpleasant slides.

There are ways in which we know ourselves better than anyone else ever could. We are the world's greatest experts on our own personal life event histories, and of course our phenomenological experiences are uniquely our own. Yet there is an aspect of our identity that is strikingly salient to others, but – under ordinary circumstances – entirely unobserved and unobservable by ourselves. This intriguing slice of the self is our own facial expressions. As we interact face-to-face with others, others can see how we appear, but we cannot. We can try to surmise what our faces might be showing by the external feedback we get from the reactions of others and by the internal feedback we receive from our own facial muscles (cf. Ekman & Friesen, 1969), but these cues are meager, indirect, and sometimes even misleading.

In our nonverbal self-awareness, then, we may be more like strangers than like inside informants (DePaulo, 1992). The literature has little to say about nonverbal self-awareness, but the hints that are available are consistent with a pessimistic view. Lanzetta and Kleck (1970), for example, videotaped men as they reacted to different colored lights that indicated that they would or would not get shocked. Then they showed the tapes to the men, and asked them to try to identify the shock and the no-shock trials. The men were no more accurate at distinguishing their own facial reactions than they were at distinguishing the reactions of other men who were strangers to them. Riggio, Widaman, and Friedman (1985) asked participants to pose six emotions and then indicate how well they thought they had sent each one. Participants' perceived sending ability was not significantly correlated with their actual sending ability. Barr and Kleck (1995) videotaped participants as they watched amusing film clips, then asked the participants how facially expressive they thought they were while watching the clips, then showed them the videotapes of their facial expressions. When participants saw their own faces on tape, they reported being surprised by how unexpressive they seemed. Further, participants' ratings of their own expressiveness before they saw the videotapes were higher than the ratings made by objective judges who had viewed the tapes. Finally, in a study of self-awareness of tone of voice, Holzman and Rousey (1966) found that people who listened to their own tape-recorded voices were surprised and not at all delighted by how they sounded.

If our inability to see our own faces as we interact with others is an important factor in our limited awareness of our own facial expressions, then it may be that people who often do see our facial expressions would be especially skilled at reading them. Perhaps those who have the most direct and plentiful experience interacting with us face-to-face, such as our close friends, are the most privileged and insightful interpreters of our facial behavior. Poets and novelists encourage us in our romantic beliefs that the people to whom we are close are so exquisitely sensitive to our thoughts and feelings that they can discern them from our nonverbal cues alone. It is surprising, then, that so far as we know, there have been no prior investigations of friends' understanding of each other's facial expressions.

There is evidence that friends are especially sensitive to each other when verbal as well as nonverbal cues are available to them. For example, pairs of friends are better than strangers at inferring each other's thoughts and feelings during their interactions with each other (Stinson & Ickes, 1992), and friends can purposefully communicate hidden messages to each other that strangers cannot discern (Fleming, Darley, Hilton, & Kojetin, 1990). These studies, though, do not tell us whether friends would be especially adept at understanding each other if they had to rely on nonverbal cues alone.

There are also reports of nonverbal sensitivity in close relationships other than friendships. It has been shown, for example, that marital partners read each other's nonverbal communications more accurately than do strangers (Sabatelli, Buck, & Dreyer, 1982) and that parents read their own children's facial expressions more accurately than other children's (Zuckerman & Przewuzman, 1979). Dating partners, however, are not better than are strangers at reading each other's facial expressions (Sabatelli, Dreyer, & Buck, 1979). And in the realm of deception, when intimates try to detect each other's lies, they sometimes show a special bias toward thinking that their partner is especially truthful, rather than showing any exceptional accuracy (e.g., McCornack & Levine, 1990).

Intuitively, a straightforward hypothesis of the effects of familiarity in nonverbal sensitivity would predict that the more experience people have had reading other people's facial expressions, the more accurate they would be. According to this hypothesis, friends would be the most accurate at reading targets' expressions relative to the targets themselves and strangers, who have had little or no experience reading the targets' expressions. However, there are some hints in the literature of a very different model of relationship effects in nonverbal sensitivity – one that predicts similarities, rather than differences, between relationship partners in their understanding of nonverbal cues.

Brauer and DePaulo (1980) found that pairs of friends were more similar to each other than were pairs of strangers in their understanding of strangers' facial expressions in a standardized test of nonverbal sensitivity. Siblings also show some similarities to each other in their perceptions of nonverbal cues (Blanck, Zuckerman, DePaulo, & Rosenthal, 1980), and husbands and wives resemble each other in their perceptions of children's facial expressions of particular affects (Zuckerman & Przewuzman, 1979). In none of these studies, however, were participants ever attempting to read their own expressions or their partner's. We think that we, too, will find similarities among friends in their reading of unfamiliar faces. In the present study, we will present the first data on whether friends are also similar to each other in their reading of familiar faces.

In this study, we examined people's skill at understanding their own facial expressions and those of their friends. We videotaped participants surreptitiously as they watched pleasant, unpleasant, and unusual slides from Buck's (1984) slide-viewing paradigm. Approximately one year later, we showed the videotapes of their facial reactions to the participants themselves, a same-sex friend, another participant who also appeared on the tape, and that other participant's friend. In an attempt to control for any effects resulting from the differential experience of the original participants and their friends (i.e., the participants gained more experience as a result of being in the study), the study was conducted a year after the original slide-viewing study and all judges in the present study were familiarized with the procedures and stimuli used in the study.

Based on an experiential hypothesis, we predicted that people would be less accurate at reading their own facial expressions than their friends would be. This hypothesis also predicts that facial expressions will be more accurately read by friends than by strangers. We also predicted that friends would resemble each other in their understanding of the expressions of unfamiliar people, and we set out to learn whether they would also resemble each other in their understanding of the faces of familiar others.

Method

Participants

Original participants. Original participants were 14 male and 14 female undergraduates who had participated in another study approximately a year earlier (DePaulo, Bell, & Witt, 1995). In the original study, the participants were videotaped without their awareness while they watched emotionally evocative slides. All of the participants from the original study whom we were able to contact agreed to participate in this study.

Friends. The 28 original participants were asked for the names of a few "same-sex close friends" so that we could invite one of them to participate. We recruited one friend of each of the original participants. All were paid $10 for their participation and the original participants were paid an extra $5 for their help in recruiting a friend.

Stimulus Materials

In the original study, participants viewed slides from a version of Buck's slide-viewing paradigm (e.g., Buck, 1984). They were videotaped without their awareness while they were alone in a room watching five pleasant (e.g., babies, pleasant scenes), five unpleasant (e.g., victims of burns, scenes from surgery), and five unusual slides (i.e., odd photographic effects), presented in one of two random orders for 10 seconds each.

The videotapes of the original participants had been edited onto master tapes such that each tape included all 15 clips from each of the 10 participants. On each tape, all of the participants were the same sex. For the purposes of the present study, we needed to recruit original participants (and their friends) in multiples of two from any master tape used in the study. If, for example, we succeeded in recruiting exactly two of the original participants on a tape plus their friends, then we could compare the first participant's reading of his or her own face (familiar target) with that participant's reading of the face of the other participant (unfamiliar target). For the second participant on the same tape and his or her friend, the comparisons would be exactly analogous. Thus, any given person on the tape was a familiar target to half of the judges (the participant him- or herself and the participant's friend) and unfamiliar to the other half (the other participant and the other participant's friend). This results in the very desirable design feature that the familiar and the unfamiliar faces do not differ in any objective way (such as in their legibility), for the faces are exactly the same, and familiarity is defined by the identity of the person who is viewing the face.

For six of the tapes (three of males and three of females), we did in fact succeed in recruiting exactly two original participants and their friends. In five other instances, we recruited three of the original participants that were on a particular tape but we were unable to recruit a fourth. Because our design required an even number of participants from each tape, we randomly excluded one participant of the three in each of these instances. Thus, our final design included 20 men (10 original participants and their friends) and 24 women (12 original participants and their friends).

Procedure

All judges were tested individually. We first described the procedure used in the original study (this was just a reminder for the original participants) and showed them photographs of the slides that the original participants had seen. These were mounted on a poster board such that all five photographs of a particular type were presented together and labeled. We told them that they would see 10-second clips of the facial expressions of 10 participants as they watched the 15 slides in a random order. Their task was to indicate each time, during the rating pause that

14

followed each clip, whether they thought the participant was viewing a pleasant, an unpleasant, or an unusual slide.

The original participants were told that their own facial expressions appeared on one of the tapes that were made from the original study, and so it was possible that they would be seeing that tape. Similarly, the friends were told that it was possible that their friend would appear on the tape. All participants were told to note if they knew anyone else on the videotape. No one reported knowing any other original participant.

Participants and their friends then completed the Berscheid, Snyder, and Omoto (1989) Relationship Closeness Inventory (RCI) which defines closeness in terms of the interdependence between relationship partners (Kelley et al., 1983). They were then debriefed, paid, and thanked for their participation.

Results

Manipulation Check: Were the Friends Close Friends?

We included the measure of relational closeness to ascertain that the partners in our study really were close friends and not just acquaintances. The scores from our sample ($M = 14.52$, $SD = 4.15$) compared very favorably to Berscheid et al.'s (1989) sample of college students reporting on the closest of all of their interpersonal relationships ($M = 12.24$, $SD = 4.29$). In addition, the pairs of friends in our sample had known each other an average of 4.06 years ($SD = 3.64$).

Measure of Nonverbal Sensitivity

One measure of nonverbal sensitivity that has often been used in the literature is a percent correct measure – e.g., what percent of the time did the judges correctly guess when the sender was viewing a pleasant slide? However, this measure cannot distinguish accuracy from a bias to report "pleasant" as an answer. Therefore, to assess judges' accuracy at identifying the types of slides that the original participants were viewing, we used an accuracy measure designed to be unaffected by response biases (Wagner, 1993). The measure is a product of the hit rate and differential accuracy. For the computation of accuracy at recognizing responses to the pleasant slides, for example, the hit rate is the number of times the judge correctly responded that the slide was pleasant, divided by the total number of times that a pleasant slide was shown. Thus, if a judge said that the participant was viewing a pleasant slide all five times that the participant actually was viewing a pleasant slide, the hit rate would be 1. Differential accuracy is the number of times the judge correctly reported that the slide was pleasant, divided by the total number of times that the judge thought that a pleasant slide was being viewed. Thus, if the judge picked pleasant as the answer only when the participant really was watching a pleasant slide, differential accuracy would be 1. The Wagner measure also includes a correction for chance. Thus, the final accuracy measure is the accuracy score minus the chance correction, after both are transformed using the arcsine transformation. Separate scores were computed to assess pleasant slide accuracy

(accuracy at recognizing when participants were viewing the pleasant slides), unpleasant, and unusual slide accuracy.

Design

The accuracy scores were the dependent measures in a mixed-design ANOVA. The units of analysis were quadrads – the two original participants who appeared on a tape, and a friend of each of those participants. Sex was the only between-groups factor. The within-groups factors were rater (original participant/friend of the original participant), familiarity of the target being rated [familiar (i.e., oneself or one's friend)/unfamiliar (i.e., a stranger)] and the order in which the target appeared on the tape (first or second). (There were no significant effects involving order.) The main effect of rater was not of interest, as it would indicate that the participants differed from their friends in their understanding of both the familiar and the unfamiliar targets. There was no reason to expect participants to be more or less accurate than their friends, and in fact they were not. With regard to the familiarity factor, the familiar target is either the rater or the rater's friend, whereas the unfamiliar target is a stranger to the rater. Therefore, a main effect of familiarity would indicate that the raters were better (or worse) at reading the familiar faces (their own faces or those of their friends) than the unfamiliar faces. Our key prediction that a target's face will be more accurately rated by the target's friend than by the target him- or herself is tested by the Rater X Familiarity of Target interaction. The predicted pattern of means would show that the degree to which the raters did better at reading the familiar faces than the unfamiliar ones was greater when the raters were the participants' friends than when they were the participants themselves.

To determine whether accuracy was significantly better than chance, we first computed preliminary ANOVAs in which a repeated measures factor with two levels was added to the basic design. The levels were accuracy uncorrected for chance and the level of accuracy that would be expected by chance (Wagner, 1993). There was a main effect of that factor in all three analyses, indicating that accuracy was significantly better than chance for pleasant, $F(1, 9) = 23.51$, $p = .001$; unpleasant, $F(1, 9) = 12.89$, $p < .01$; and unusual slides, $F(1, 9) = 5.72$, $p = .04$.

Are Friends More Advantaged at Reading the Participants' Expressions Than the Participants Are Themselves?

The Rater X Familiarity interaction was not significant for any of the accuracy scores. For pleasant and unusual accuracy, the *F*s for this effect were essentially zero, $F(1, 9) = .25$ and $F(1, 9) = .00$, respectively. For unpleasant accuracy, the $F(1, 9)$ was 1.99, raising at least the possibility that with a more powerful design (e.g., one with more participants), the interaction would have been significant. However, the means were not even in the predicted direction. In sum, there was no evidence for a Rater X Familiarity interaction. Further, the interaction of this effect with sex was also nonsignificant for all three accuracy measures (all *F*s < 1).

16

There were also no significant main effects for familiarity, indicating that raters (both participants and friends) did no better at reading familiar faces than unfamiliar ones. However, for pleasant accuracy, there was an unanticipated Sex X Familiarity interaction, $F(1, 9) = 6.53$, $p < .05$. In the male dyads, raters were relatively more accurate at reading the familiar faces ($M = .63$) than the unfamiliar ones ($M = .36$), whereas in the female dyads, raters were relatively more accurate at reading the unfamiliar faces ($M = .58$) than the familiar ones ($M = .49$). Protected t tests (Fisher LSD) indicated that the men were significantly more accurate at reading the familiar faces than the unfamiliar ones, $t(9) = 2.69$, $p < .05$, but the women were not significantly less accurate at reading the familiar faces than the unfamiliar ones, $t < 1$. Consistent with previous research (e.g., Hall, 1984), decoding accuracy was greater for the female dyads than the male dyads when the raters were judging strangers, $t(9) = 2.19$, $p = .056$. However, when the face was familiar to the raters, ability to decode the facial expressions was not significantly different in the female dyads than in the male dyads, $t(9) = 1.40$.[1] Thus, it appears that women do not outperform men when reading familiar, same-sex people reacting to pleasant slides. The results suggest that familiarity enhances men's accuracy, allowing the men to match the decoding abilities of women.

The fact that only the Sex X Familiarity interaction was significant, and the three-way interaction of those two variables with rater was not, indicates that the participants and their friends did not differ in the degree to which they were better or worse at reading the familiar faces than the unfamiliar faces. For the men, the friends did better at reading facial reactions to the pleasant slides when the faces they were reading were those of their friends than of strangers. This finding by itself is consistent with an experiential hypothesis about nonverbal sensitivity. However, the participants *also* did better at reading their own faces than the faces of strangers, and the degree to which they were advantaged was no less than it was for their friends. For women, familiarity was no help to either the participants themselves or their friends.

Within sex, differences in accuracy as a function of familiarity cannot be accounted for by any objective differences in facial expressions, because the familiar faces and the unfamiliar ones were actually the exact same faces. For every videotape, all faces were rated by all raters. Any particular face was familiar to exactly half of the judges who viewed it (the participant him/herself and the participant's friend) and unfamiliar to the other half (the other participant and the other participant's friend). For men, then, facial reactions to the pleasant slides were more identifiable as such to the men themselves and to their friends than they were to strangers; for the women, no differences were found.

Of course, it is possible that the men's facial expressions differed in important ways from the women's. Much previous research (see DePaulo, 1992; Hall, 1984; and Manstead, 1991, for reviews) suggests that men's expressions are often less clear than women's.[2] This could account for any overall differences in the readability of the men's and the women's faces. However, if it were only objective differences between men's and women's facial expressions that influenced raters' accuracy, then the differences in decoding ability between the male dyads and the female dyads should have been exactly the same in size and direction for the familiar faces as for the unfamiliar ones. (Again, this is so because of the important design feature that within sex, the

17

familiar faces and the unfamiliar ones were actually the exact same faces.) Instead, decoding ability was significantly better in the female dyads than in the male dyads only if the faces were unfamiliar to the raters.[3]

Do Friends Interpret Facial Expressions More Similarly Than Do Strangers?

Table 1 shows the intraclass correlations testing the similarity of pairs of friends relative to pairs of strangers for both the males and the females. The female friends showed significant or nearly significant similarity in their reading of both familiar and unfamiliar faces for pleasant, unpleasant, and unusual accuracy. In fact, the mean of the three correlations for the reading of unfamiliar faces was .62, a value strikingly similar to the .64 reported by Brauer and DePaulo (1980) in their study in which female friends read unfamiliar faces (see Table 1).

For male friends, however, the results were very different. Five of the six intraclass correlations were nonsignificant. Only in their reading of strangers' reactions to unpleasant slides did male friends show any similarity in nonverbal decoding accuracy.

Table 1

Friends' Similarity in Their Understanding of the Facial Expressions of Familiar and Unfamiliar People: Intraclass Correlations

	Accuracy Type		
Sex	**Pleasant**	**Unpleasant**	**Unusual**
Males (n = 10 pairs)			
Familiar	-.16	-.15	.37
Unfamiliar	.07	.93***	.23
Females (n = 12 pairs)			
Familiar	.60*	.78**	.57+
Unfamiliar	.80**	.56+	.50+
Z,			
Females minus males[a]			
Familiar	1.70+	2.37*	.51
Unfamiliar	2.04*	-2.04*	.63

[a]The *Z*s reported here test the differences in the correlations between the males and the females.
+$p < .10$. *$p < .05$. **$p < .01$. ***$p < .001$.

18

Discussion

Did Familiarity Enhance Understanding?

We predicted that people would be less astute at reading their own facial expressions than their friends would be, because their friends have the advantage of seeing those facial expressions during many social interactions. We found no support for this prediction. Instead, the patterns of sensitivities and insensitivities that people showed in reading their own faces exactly paralleled those of their friends.

We also predicted that people's facial expressions would be more accurately read by their friends than by strangers. Generally, we were wrong about this, too. The one exception was that men's facial reactions to the pleasant slides were more accurately recognized by their friends than by strangers. However, those reactions were also more accurately recognized by the men themselves than by strangers. Once again, then, the men and their friends showed the same mean differences and similarities in their sensitivities to nonverbal cues.

Why is it that the raters showed virtually no special sensitivity to their friends' facial expressions? We suspect that when the raters in the present study went astray in their interpretations of their friends' facial reactions, they did so in part because they did not fully appreciate the fact that they have an important impact on their friends' facial expressions, and that their friends might act very differently when they are alone (e.g., Buck, Losow, Murphy, & Costanzo, 1992). Perhaps, then, if we had shown our raters videotapes from times when they were interacting with their friends, they would have been more insightful in their interpretations of their friends' facial expressions. But if people do in fact show special sensitivity only to the expressions that they see in their friends during their own personal interactions with them, then their understanding of their friends is not broad and deep, but instead rather circumscribed (Swann, 1984).

Do Friends Resemble Each Other in their Sensitivity to Facial Expressions?

The Brauer and DePaulo (1980) finding that female friends were more similar to each other than were pairs of strangers in their reading of a stranger's facial expressions set the empirical precedent for our own findings. We expected the friends in our study to be more similar than the negligible similarity expected for strangers in their reading of unfamiliar faces. For the female friends, they were: Women and their friends tended to be uniquely linked to each other in their ability to recognize strangers' reactions to emotionally evocative slides. They showed striking resemblances in nonverbal skill.

When pairs of friends observe the faces of strangers, they often share a similar (visual) point of view. But one friend's view of the other friend's facial expressions is very different from the friend's (lack of) view of his or her own expressions. Therefore, it would have been entirely plausible to find no similarities between friends in their understanding of the familiar faces. But instead, for the women, we found that pairs of friends showed impressive resemblances in their understanding of the familiar faces. Women who were very sensitive to their own facial expressions had friends who were also sensitive to those expressions, whereas women who were very inaccurate readers of their own faces had friends who were similarly poor at reading those expressions.

In contrast, male friends were generally no more similar than what would be expected for pairs of male strangers in their perceptions of any of the facial expressions. The one (unanticipated) exception was that pairs of male friends were strikingly similar to each other in their reading of the reactions to the unpleasant slides of the men who were strangers to them. That men and their friends showed such limited resemblances to each other is especially noteworthy in view of the resemblances in other close relationships that have already been documented. In addition to the findings of similarities among female friends (Brauer & DePaulo, 1980, and now this study), there have been reports that both siblings (Blanck et al., 1980) and marital partners (Zuckerman & Przewuzman, 1979) resemble each other in their reading of facial expressions that are not their own.

Our finding that female friends show similarities in nonverbal accuracy and male friends generally do not, has an intriguing parallel in the study of personality perception. Kenny and Kashy (1995) studied men and women who lived in same-sex residential groups (e.g., college fraternities and sororities) and were acquainted with all of the people in their group. They found that pairs of close friends within the groups agreed with each other in their perceptions of the personality traits of the other group members. The friends were especially similar in their unique perceptions of other people (i.e., specific ways of viewing particular people that were different from their usual ways of viewing others). Importantly, pairs of female friends were much more likely to show this similarity in their unique perceptions of others than were pairs of male friends.

We do not think that male friends have no special attunement to each other. In a very different kind of paradigm, Stinson and Ickes (1992) videotaped pairs of male friends and male strangers interacting with each other, and then asked each person about the other person's thoughts and feelings during the interaction. The resulting empathy scores were more highly correlated for the pairs of friends than for the pairs of strangers. This means that male friends are matched in their empathy for each other. However, this is a different kind of finding from the Kenny and Kashy (1995) finding, and our own finding that male friends are less similar to each other than female friends in accuracy in understanding their nonverbal cues.

We do not know whether friends' similarity to each other in their reading of nonverbal cues is a cause, a consequence, or merely a correlate of their friendship with each other. The "cause" hypothesis suggests that people seek as friends those who see the world similarly. To women, the

20

sharing of this interpretive lens may be broadly important, whereas to men, perhaps it is only the sharing of interpretations of reactions that are emotionally significant to them – such as other men's reactions to distress – that are of sufficient import to form the foundation for a friendship (see also Ickes, Tooke, Stinson, Baker, & Bissonnette, 1988).

The "consequence" hypothesis suggests that as the friendship develops, friends become more similar to each other in their social interpretations. One possible mechanism for this growing similarity is simply talking. For example, Deutsch, Sullivan, Sage, and Basile (1991) found that female friends who talked to each other more shared more overlap in the traits that they ascribed to themselves (see also Brauer & DePaulo, 1980). Talking and emotional sharing are generally more important to women's same-sex friendships than to men's (e.g., Sherrod, 1989).

Another possibility is that friends' interpretive similarities are rooted in the co-orientation of their attention. Friends may be especially similar in how they interpret social cues when they are especially similar in the social cues to which they attend. Male friends may resemble each other in the degree to which they orient to men's reactions to distress. Female friends may be more generally similar to each other in the distribution of their attention in their interpersonal lives.

Sex Differences in Nonverbal Sensitivity Revisited

The cultural wisdom that women are more nonverbally sensitive than men has been echoed empirically by dozens of studies showing that women do in fact read other people's nondeceptive expressions of emotion more accurately than do men (e.g., Hall, 1984; but see DePaulo, Epstein, & Wyer, 1993, and Rosenthal & DePaulo, 1979, for sex differences in reading more covert cues). That literature, however, has been based almost entirely on the reading of the nonverbal communication of strangers. In the present study, we also found that when the facial expressions our participants were reading were those of unfamiliar people watching pleasant slides, decoding accuracy was better in the female dyads than in the male dyads. However, when the faces were instead familiar ones – the judge's own face or the face of a friend – decoding accuracy in the female dyads was no different from the male dyads. The implications that women may have no special advantage over men in reading people who are familiar to them, or put another way, that men have abilities equal to those of women at reading familiar people, should be pursued in studies in which men and women have both male and female friends in common. That way, men and women can be compared when they are reading the exact same facial expressions, and their accuracy at reading same-sex familiar and unfamiliar people can be compared to their accuracy at reading opposite-sex people.

Notes

1. In an analysis of the incorrect responses, we found that when the raters guessed wrong about the participants who were actually viewing the pleasant slides, they guessed that the participants were viewing unusual slides significantly more often than unpleasant ones, Ms = 1.71 and 1.09, $F(1, 9)$ = 12.01, $p < .01$. This effect, however, did not interact significantly with any other variable, all $Fs < 1$.

2. In this study at least, they did not seem to be less pleasant. When we analyzed the total number of times across all 15 slides that the raters thought that the participants were viewing a pleasant slide, there were no significant effects involving sex.

3. We also conducted the ANOVAs using the traditional percent accuracy measure. The one effect relevant to familiarity effects that was significant using the Wagner (1993) measure – Sex X Familiarity for pleasantness accuracy – was nearly significant for the percent accuracy measure, $F(1, 9)$ = 4.36, $p = .07$. The two measures were also similar in that, with one exception, they produced no other effects involving familiarity for any of the variables. The one exception was the main effect of familiarity for unusual accuracy. It was significant for the percent accuracy measure, $F(1, 9)$ = 8.70, $p = .02$, Ms = 50% and 41% respectively for the familiar and unfamiliar faces (chance is 33%), but not for the Wagner (1993) measure, $F(1, 9)$ = 1.64, $p = .23$. According to the logic of the Wagner measure, this discrepancy could occur if raters guessed "unusual" too often when rating the familiar faces. As a result, the raters would appear to be accurate according to the percent accuracy measure, which does not correct for the fact that raters might select the answer "unusual" when the facial expressions were *not* reactions to the unusual slides as well as when they were. To examine this further, we recomputed the ANOVA using the number of times raters picked "unusual" as our dependent measure. Although the main effect of familiarity was not significant, $F(1, 9)$ = 1.35, $p = .28$, the means were in the expected direction. Raters guessed "unusual" more often when they were judging familiar faces ($M = 6.0$) than unfamiliar ones ($M = 5.5$). It is also worth noting that raters were picking "unusual" more often than they should have; only five of the 15 slides really were unusual, but raters chose unusual as their answer more than five times.

References

Barr, C. L., & Kleck, R. E. (1995). Self/other perceptions of the intensity of facial expression of emotion: Do we know what we show? *Journal of Personality and Social Psychology, 68,* 608-618.

Berscheid, E., Snyder, M., & Omoto, A. M. (1989). The Relationship Closeness Inventory: Assessing the closeness of interpersonal relationships. *Journal of Personality and Social Psychology, 57,* 792-807.

Blanck, P. D., Zuckerman, M., DePaulo, B. M., & Rosenthal, R. (1980). Sibling resemblances in nonverbal skill and style. *Journal of Nonverbal Behavior, 4,* 219-226.

Brauer, D. V., & DePaulo, B. M. (1980). Similarities between friends in their understanding of nonverbal cues. *Journal of Nonverbal Behavior*, *5*, 64-68.

Buck, R. (1984). *The communication of emotion*. New York: Guilford Press.

Buck, R., Losow, J. I., Murphy, M. M., & Costanzo, P. (1992). Social facilitation and inhibition of emotional expression and communication. *Journal of Personality and Social Psychology*, *63*, 962-968.

DePaulo, B. M. (1992). Nonverbal behavior and self-presentation. *Psychological Bulletin*, *111*, 203-243.

DePaulo, B. M., Bell, K. L., & Witt, C. L. (1995). Feigning spontaneity. Research in progress.

DePaulo, B. M., Epstein, J. A., & Wyer, M. M. (1993). Sex differences in lying: How women and men deal with the dilemma of deceit. In M. Lewis & C. Saarni (Eds.), *Lying and deception in everyday life* (pp. 126-147). New York: Guilford.

Deutsch, F. M., Sullivan, L., Sage, C., & Basile, N. (1991). The relations among talking, liking, and similarity between friends. *Personality and Social Psychology Bulletin*, *17*, 406-411.

Ekman, P., & Friesen, W. V. (1969). Nonverbal leakage and clues to deception. *Psychiatry*, *32*, 88-106.

Fleming, J. H., Darley, J. M., Hilton, J. L., & Kojetin, B. A. (1990). Multiple audience problem: A strategic communication perspective on social perception. *Journal of Personality and Social Psychology*, *58*, 593-609.

Hall, J. A. (1984). *Nonverbal sex differences: Communication accuracy and expressive style*. Baltimore: Johns Hopkins University Press.

Holzman, P. S., & Rousey, C. (1966). The voice as pecept. *Journal of Personality and Social Psychology*, *4*, 78-86.

Ickes, W., Tooke, W., Stinson, L., Baker, V. L., & Bissonnette, V. (1988). Naturalistic social cognition: Intersubjectivity in same-sex dyads. *Journal of Nonverbal Behavior*, *12*, 58-84.

Kelley, H. H., Berscheid, E., Christensen, A., Harvey, J. H., Huston, T. L., Levinger, G., McClintock, E., Peplau, L. A., & Peterson, D. R. (1983). *Close relationships*. New York: Freeman.

Kenny, D. A., & Kashy, D. A. (1995). Enhanced coorientation in the perceptions of friends: A social relations analysis. *Journal of Personality and Social Psychology*, *67*, 1024-1033.

Lanzetta, J. T., & Kleck, R. E. (1970). Encoding and decoding nonverbal affect in humans. *Journal of Personality and Social Psychology*, *16*, 12-19.

Manstead, A. S. R. (1991). Expressiveness as an individual difference. In R. S. Feldman & B. Rime (Eds.), *Fundamentals of nonverbal behavior* (pp. 285-328). Cambridge: Cambridge University Press.

McCornack, S. A., & Levine, T. R. (1990). When lovers become leery: The relationship between suspicion and accuracy in detecting deception. *Communication Monographs*, *57*, 219-230.

Riggio, R. E., Widaman, K. F., & Friedman, H. S. (1985). Actual and perceived emotional sending and personality correlates. *Journal of Nonverbal Behavior, 9*, 69-83.

Rosenthal, R., & DePaulo, B. M. (1979). Sex differences in eavesdropping on nonverbal cues. *Journal of Personality and Social Psychology, 37*, 273-285.

Sabatelli, R. M., Buck, R., & Dreyer, A. (1982). Nonverbal communication accuracy in married couples: Relationship with marital complaints. *Journal of Personality and Social Psychology, 43*, 1088-1097.

Sabatelli, R. M., Dreyer, A., & Buck, R. (1979). Cognitive style and sending and receiving of facial cues. *Perceptual and Motor Skills, 49*, 203-212.

Sherrod, D. (1989). The influence of gender on same-sex friendships. In C. Hendrick (Ed.), *Review of personality and social psychology: Vol 10, Close relationships* (pp. 164-186). Newbury Park, CA: Sage.

Stinson, L., & Ickes, W. (1992). Empathic accuracy in the interactions of male friends versus male strangers. *Journal of Personality and Social Psychology, 62*, 787-797.

Swann, W. B. (1984). Quest for accuracy in person perception: A matter of pragmatics. *Psychological Review, 91*, 457-477.

Wagner, H. L. (1993). On measuring performance in category judgment studies of nonverbal behavior. *Journal of Nonverbal Behavior, 17*, 3-28.

Wagner, H. L., Lewis, H., Ramsay, S., & Krediet, I. (1992). Predictions of facial displays from knowledge of norms of emotional expressiveness. *Motivation and Emotion, 16*, 347-362.

Zuckerman, M., & Przewuzman, S. J. (1979). Decoding and encoding facial expressions in preschool-age children. *Environmental Psychology and Nonverbal Behavior, 3*, 147-163.

Journal of Nonverbal Behavior, 19(3), Fall 1995
@ 1995 Human Sciences Press, Inc.

Journal of Nonverbal Behavior, 2004, *24*, 245-266.

Reading Nonverbal Cues to Emotions:
The Advantages and Liabilities of Relationship Closeness

R. Weylin Sternglanz and Bella M. DePaulo

Accuracy at reading nonverbal cues to emotions was examined for close friends, less close friends, and strangers. Forty-eight senders were videotaped talking about an experience during which they felt either very happy, very sad, or very angry. Half of the time they expressed their emotion clearly, and half of the time they concealed their emotion. Forty-eight judges watched these tapes without sound and attempted to identify the senders' emotions. Each judge watched a videotape of both a platonic friend and a stranger. Overall, friends were more accurate than strangers at identifying the senders' emotions; however, less close friends were better than closer friends at correctly judging concealed sadness and anger. In discussing these findings, we consider models of motivated inaccuracy, accommodatingness, and emotions as calls to action.

Decoding Nonverbal Cues to Emotions: The Advantages and Liabilities of Closeness

Conventional wisdom suggests that we are best at reading the nonverbal cues of those people who are closest to us. This accuracy could be a straightforward consequence of having greater practice and experience with a close relationship partner's nonverbal cues. Close relationship partners obviously know more about each others' lives than strangers, and should have some experience observing each other's idiosyncratic reactions to different situations. In fact, there is some evidence to support this intuitive hypothesis. Romantic partners (Noller & Ruzzene, 1991; Sabatelli, Buck, & Dreyer, 1982) and friends (Fleming, Darley, Hilton, & Kojetin, 1990; Stinson & Ickes, 1992) are better at reading each other's cues than are strangers, and parents read the facial expressions of their own children more accurately than those of other children (Zuckerman & Przewuzman, 1979).

The preponderance of the evidence (reviewed by Ickes & Simpson, 1997) also supports a second intuitively compelling hypothesis: Interpersonal understanding of emotions can be good for relationships. For example, happier couples have more accurate understandings of their partners' negative thoughts and feelings during periods of conflict (Knudson, Sommers, & Golding, 1980; Noller & Ruzzene, 1991), whereas unhappy romantic partners often misunderstand each other's emotions (Gottman, 1979). Similarly, college roommates who are skillful readers of nonverbal cues feel more positively about their interactions with each other than pairs of roommates who are less nonverbally sensitive (Hodgins & Zuckerman, 1990).

Liabilities of Closeness in Reading Nonverbal Cues

As the study of relationships has progressed, it has become evident that nonverbal sensitivity is neither an inevitable concomitant of relationship familiarity nor even necessarily an advantageous one. For example, there are indications that friends and dating partners generally are no more insightful than strangers at understanding each other's facial expressions (Ansfield, DePaulo, & Bell, 1995; Sabatelli, Dreyer, & Buck, 1979). In fact, in many instances, people are no better than strangers at interpreting even their own videotaped facial expressions (Ansfield et al., 1995).

Why should there be exceptions to the seemingly intuitive relationship between closeness and nonverbal sensitivity? Although greater closeness is linked with greater knowledge of the other person and practice at reading their cues, it is also tied to greater investment (cf. Sillars, 1985). People in close relationships have a stake in positive perceptions. These include perceptions of their partners, beliefs about their partners' perceptions of them, and, of course, perceptions of the relationship itself. In reasonable doses, these positive illusions (perceptions that are more positive than may be warranted) seem to contribute to relationship stability and satisfaction (e.g., Ickes & Simpson, 1997; Murray & Holmes, 1999; Murray, Holmes, & Griffin, 1996; Sillars, Pike, Jones, & Murphy, 1984).

Positive illusions about the honesty of relationship partners are well documented. Relationship partners see more of each others' communications as truthful than do pairs of strangers (e.g., Anderson, Ansfield, & DePaulo, 1999). Because close relationship partners tell everyday lies at a lower rate than do strangers (DePaulo & Kashy, 1998), perhaps these differential perceptions of honesty are not actually illusory. But even when people tell truths and lies to their relationship partners and to strangers at the same time, relationship partners, more often than strangers, believe that the honest and the dishonest communications are truthful (e.g., Anderson, 1999).

Perceptions of honesty are good candidates for positive illusions because of the reassurance afforded by the belief that one's relationship partners are people who do not tell lies. Perceptions of partners' feelings or emotions may also be likely candidates. Partners' feelings of anger, frustration, and dissatisfaction, if accurately identified, could threaten perceivers' views of these partners, their beliefs about how the partners view them, and their faith in the relationship. These negative emotions may also be more hurtful to perceivers when expressed by close relationship partners than by strangers (e.g., Whitesell & Harter, 1996).

There is comfort, then, in overlooking certain emotions expressed by relationship partners. There is also a behavioral risk to noticing demeaning and destructive affects communicated by relationship partners: It can be very tempting to respond in kind. When that impulse is indulged, the relationship is likely to suffer (Rusbult, Johnson, & Morrow, 1986; Rusbult, Verette, Whitney, Slovik, & Lipkus, 1991; see also Gottman, 1979). In her program of research on accommodative processes in close relationships, Rusbult and her colleagues have emphasized the value of inhibiting the impulse to respond to unkind cuts with searing barbs of one's own.

However, that can require more effort and virtue than many ordinary mortals can muster in the heat of hostilities. It may be simpler not to notice the expressions of negativity in the first place.

Obliviousness, though, has its limits. Causes of anger that could have been addressed may instead fester and ultimately poison the relationship. Insensitivity to a partner's anger may itself compound that anger, adding the insult of being ignored to the original injury caused by the anger-triggering offence. Consequently, perceivers who completely miss their partners' simmering rage may soon find that rage exploding rather than dissipating (Tavris, 1982). Further, inaccuracy is not always a plausible option; emotions that are very clearly expressed cannot easily be misinterpreted or ignored.

Ickes and Simpson (1997) have developed a model of motivated inaccuracy in which the clarity of the cues to the partners' thoughts and feelings is one of the most important predictors. Motivated inaccuracy is most likely to occur when cues are ambiguous, because ambiguity allows the perceiver to entertain a wide range of plausible interpretations. Another predictor in the model that is at least as important as ambiguity is the nature and potential implications of the partner's actual thoughts and feelings. To the degree that an accurate reading of those cues would be threatening to the perceiver or to the relationship, the more motivated the perceiver will be to misinterpret them. The potential for threat, then, sets the motivational stage, and ambiguity allows the play of inaccuracy to proceed.

The Ickes and Simpson (1997) model gives the leading role to the perceiver's own feelings of threat. An alternative (though not mutually exclusive) script casts the sender as the main character. In this interpretation, cues can be ambiguous because the person expressing them wants them to be. Perceivers who read the cues that others are deliberately trying to conceal may be committing a particularly baleful violation of polite behavior (Rosenthal & DePaulo, 1979). Rosenthal and DePaulo (1979) showed that women, more so than men, seem to avoid reading cues that others are trying to hide from them. In those studies, however, all of the communications were among strangers. Close relationship partners may not feel similarly obligated to respect each other's emotional privacy when the concealed information may be relevant to their own concerns or to the fate of the relationship (e.g., Anderson, DePaulo, & Ansfield, 2002).

In the present study, we directly manipulated the clarity of nonverbal cues to emotions by asking participants to express their emotions clearly in some of their communications and to conceal them in others. We then examined the accuracy of relationship partners and strangers at reading those cues. We selected three emotions that we expected to vary in the degree to which they could prove threatening to the perceivers: happiness, sadness, and anger.

The study of positive illusions and motivated inaccuracy has to this point focused almost exclusively on romantic partners. However, close friends may also be motivated to overlook threatening emotions (Whitesell & Harter, 1996). In the present study, we examined platonic

27

friends. Unlike any investigation of interpersonal sensitivity between friends of which we are aware, our study included both same-sex and opposite-sex platonic friends.

Decoding Different Emotions: The Special Case of Anger

If close relationship partners do learn to overlook certain cues, they are likely to do so with some emotions more than others. The ramifications of recognizing anger, for instance, should often be more treacherous than the ramifications of accurately reading happiness or sadness (Coats & Feldman, 1996; Rotter & Rotter, 1988;). The ability to identify anger may have a unique function, as it is the emotion most likely to be threatening either to a social interaction, a relationship, or to the perceivers themselves.

Sociobiologists posit that the communication of anger is particularly valuable for men, as a means of advancing within the dominance hierarchy without resorting to outright aggression (De Waal, 1996). The available evidence, which is based on communications between strangers, is consistent with this claim. Although women are generally better than men at expressing their emotions clearly with nonverbal cues (e.g, Hall, 1984,1987), and at recognizing other people's nonverbal expressions of emotions (Hall, 1984, 1987), they are not superior to men at communicating anger. Men's anger is expressed more clearly than women's (e.g., Bonebright, Thompson, and Leger, 1996; Coats & Feldman, 1996; Rotter & Rotter, 1988) and men are better than women at reading anger in others (Wagner, MacDonald, & Manstead, 1986), especially other men (Rotter & Rotter, 1988).

The relationship implications of expressing anger clearly also appear to be different for men than for women. Men whose facial expressions of anger are more easily recognized have greater sociometric status among their fellow fraternity members. For women, popularity among their sorority sisters is negligibly related to the clarity of their expressions of anger, but it is related to the readability of their facial expressions of happiness (Coats & Feldman, 1996). Even in this study, however, the criterion for legibility of facial expressions was the accuracy of strangers (and not the fellow fraternity or sorority members) at identifying the emotions.

The communication of emotions among strangers, however, is less fraught with significant relationship implications than is the communication among friends, lovers, or family members, and the dynamics may differ, too (e.g., Buck, Losow, Murphy, & Costanzo, 1992; DePaulo, 1992; Schlenker & Britt, 2001; Tice, Butler, Muraven, & Stillwell, 1995; Wagner & Smith, 1991). Whether there will be sex differences in the degree to which relationship partners tune in to threatening cues or tune them out remains to be seen.

Predictions

Our clearest predictions about the differences in the nonverbal sensitivity between strangers and friends are for emotions that are expressed clearly. In the reading of those communications, friends will have the advantage of practice, experience, and knowledge about their partners, and will therefore interpret the cues more accurately. For the deliberately concealed emotions, we generated competing predictions. From a motivated inaccuracy perspective, we predicted that relationship partners (more so than strangers) would feel threatened by the other person's feelings of anger, and perhaps also sadness, but not by their feelings of happiness. The ambiguity of cues that results from attempts at concealment would allow them to misinterpret those cues. Therefore, relationship partners will be less accurate than strangers at reading concealed cues to negative emotions, but not positive ones. Alternatively, relationship partners may be especially advantaged over strangers in reading cues to concealed emotions because they are less likely to believe that emotions should be hidden from them, and because their greater experience may be necessary for the accurate identification of suppressed and ambiguous cues. The alternative hypothesis is intuitively compelling; nevertheless, the literature on motivated inaccuracy does not support it.

Another set of predictions, regarding sex differences, was derived from past research and theory. However, the previous work was based on communications among strangers, so its extension to communications among friends is in question. Specifically, we predicted that women's nonverbal expressions of emotions would be more accurately read than men's, and that women would read other people's nonverbal expressions of emotions more accurately than would men. However, women's advantage over men in decoding emotions may be evident only for the cues that senders want the perceivers to see (the emotions that are expressed clearly), and not the emotions that senders are attempting to hide (Rosenthal & DePaulo, 1979). Finally, in both the expression and recognition of anger, men may be more successful than women.

Method

Overview

A pair of platonic friends participated in each session. Half of the participants (one from each pair) were "senders" who were videotaped speaking about experiences during which they felt happiness, sadness, and anger. In one set of communications, senders were instructed to conceal their emotions as they described their experiences; in another set, senders were instructed to express their emotions clearly. The other half of the participants ("judges") watched these tapes without sound and attempted to identify the senders' emotions. Each judge watched a videotape of both a friend and a stranger.

Participants

Forty-eight undergraduate dyads at the University of Virginia, each consisting of a pair of platonic friends, participated in the study. One of the participants from each dyad was enrolled in an introductory psychology course. When potential participants were contacted, they were randomly assigned to bring with them either a male or a female platonic friend they had known for at least three months. The introductory psychology student was designated as the sender, and

29

the student's friend was assigned to be the judge. Participants either received credit toward the fulfillment of a requirement of the psychology course, or if not enrolled in the course, they received seven dollars. There were four different types of dyads (12 of each type): a male sender and male judge; a female sender and female judge; a female sender and male judge; and a male sender and female judge.

Procedure

The two friends in each dyad arrived at the study together. After the participants signed consent forms, the experimenter confirmed that the two participants had indeed been friends for at least three months, but were not romantically involved. At this point, one participant was designated the "sender" and the other participant was designated the "judge." The judge was asked to go to another room to fill out a series of questionnaires regarding his or her friendship with the sender, including the Relationship Closeness Inventory (RCI; Berscheid, Snyder, & Omoto, 1989). The sender was seated in front of a video camera, and was told that he or she would be asked to speak about an experience in which someone made him or her feel either very happy, very sad, or very angry. In the first set of communications, the sender was either instructed to express his/her emotions clearly in all three emotion stories (happy, sad, and angry), or was instructed to conceal his/her emotions in all three stories. In the second set of communications, the sender described the same happy, sad, and angry events, but this time the sender concealed his/her emotions (if he/she had expressed them clearly previously) or expressed them clearly (if he/she had concealed them previously). Thus, all participants related a total of six stories: a happy, sad, and angry experience in which the participant's emotions were expressed clearly; and a happy, sad, and angry experience in which the participant's emotions were disguised. The order of expressing versus concealing was counterbalanced, as was the sequence of the three emotion types within each set. Senders were videotaped telling all six stories. The instructions given to participants prior to each story were identical except for those parts related to the emotion participants were asked to recall.

The instructions included the following:

> Try to think of an experience you've had in which someone made you feel very [happy/ sad/angry]. Try to recall all that you can about what happened during that experience, and exactly how you felt at that time. Keep in mind that this does not necessarily need to be an experience during which you [laughed out loud and jumped for joy/ broke down crying/ yelled or acted aggressively] (although you may have!) What is important is that ["happy"/ "sad"/ "angry"] is the emotion that best describes how this person made you feel.

When participants were instructed to *express their emotions clearly*, they heard the following instructions:

As you tell this story, try to relive it in your mind. Tell what happened that made you feel so [happy/sad/angry]. Try to feel the [happiness/sadness/anger] all over again. Don't hold back from expressing that [happiness/sadness/anger]. Tell your story so that it would be obvious to anyone watching you that this experience made you [happy/sad/angry]. Someone watching you should be able to tell that this experience made you [happy/sad/angry] even if they could not hear your words. Be as clear as you possibly can about how this experience made you feel.

When participants were instructed to *conceal* their emotions, they heard the following instructions:

As you tell this story, try to relive it in your mind. Tell what happened that made you feel so [happy/sad/angry]. However, try not to seem outwardly [happy/sad/angry]. Tell your story in such a way that it would NOT be obvious to someone watching you that the experience made you [happy/sad/angry]. Someone watching you who could NOT hear your words should NOT be able to tell just from watching you that you were feeling any particular emotion. Try to hide how this experience made you feel.

As the sender told each of his or her stories, the experimenter sat behind a partition to minimize any influence on the sender's nonverbal expressions. After each story, the participant reported on 9-point scales the intensity of the happiness, sadness, and anger they felt during the telling of the experience.

After completing the story telling, the sender filled out the same friendship questionnaires the judge had answered previously. During that time, the judge watched a tape of a sender from a previous session (who was always a stranger to the judge), as well a tape of the sender from the current session (who was the judge's friend). The tape of the stranger was from the most recently run prior session in which the gender of both the sender and judge were the same as in the current session.[1] The tapes of the stranger and of the friend were presented to the judge without sound. The order in which the two tapes were judged was counterbalanced. Immediately after viewing each emotion story told by either a stranger or a friend, the judge indicated his or her judgement as to the type of emotional event the sender had discussed (happy, sad, angry, or the false option 'neutral'). Upon completing this task, both the sender and judge were thanked for their participation, paid or given class credit, and debriefed.

Results

Manipulation Checks

Senders' ratings of the intensity of their happiness, sadness, anger, embarrassment, relaxation, and comfort, made after each of their stories, served as manipulation checks to ensure that senders actually experienced the intended emotions. The midpoint of the scales ("5") indicated a neutral rating of the emotion. Participants reported experiencing levels of happiness significantly higher than the midpoint after telling a happy story ($M = 7.38$), $t(47) = 13.7$, $p < .001$; significantly sadder than the midpoint after telling a sad story ($M = 6.32$), $t(47) = 5.77$, $p < .001$; and significantly angrier than the midpoint after telling an angry story ($M = 6.17$), $t(47) = 4.94$, $p < .001$.

We also tested whether senders experienced the relevant emotion to a greater degree than the other emotions with an analysis in which the three key emotion ratings (happiness, sadness, and anger) were levels of a repeated measures factor. When senders had told a happy story the contrast weights were +2 for happiness and -1 for sadness and anger. This contrast was significant, $F(1, 440) = 246.09$, $p < .001$, indicating that senders reported experiencing greater levels of happiness than any of the other emotions. They also reported experiencing significantly greater levels of sadness than any of the other emotions after telling a sad story, $F(1, 440) = 58.41$, $p < .001$; and significantly greater levels of anger than any of the other emotions after telling an angry story, $F(1, 440) = 46.53$, $p < .001$.

Design

Judges were the units of analysis in a mixed-design ANOVA. Judges' accuracy at decoding the emotional content of senders' stories was the dependent measure. Judges were assigned a score of "0" if their perception was incorrect and "1" if it was correct (see Rosenthal & Rosnow, 1991; Snedecor & Cochran, 1967; and Winer, 1971, for use of ANOVA with dichotomous dependent variables). The repeated measures variables were the emotional content of the senders' stories (happy, sad, and angry), the expressiveness of the senders' stories (expressed clearly vs. concealed), and the relationship between the sender and the judge (friend vs. stranger). Between-judge variables were the sex of the sender and the sex of the judge.

Accuracy or bias?

One difficulty in interpreting judges' emotion guesses is the possibility that the scores we computed may have assessed bias instead of (or in addition to) accuracy. By the procedure of assigning a score of "0" if the judge's perception was incorrect or "1" if it was correct, accurate judges of (for example) anger would earn high accuracy scores, but so would judges who were simply biased to choose anger, and who often chose anger even when the story was happy or sad. Wagner (1993) addressed this problem by creating a measure he calls the *unbiased hit rate*, designed specifically (though not exclusively) for studies of nonverbal behavior. This measure controls statistically for judges' response biases; in other words, the unbiased hit rate takes into account not only the proportion of times judges correctly identify an emotion, but also any bias judges have toward choosing a particular emotion. The unbiased hit rate ranges from 0 to 1 (or 0% to 100%), and so is easily interpretable and allows for comparison across studies. We therefore used unbiased hit rates (with arcsine transformations) as our measures of accuracy in all of our analyses. The unbiased hit rates are the scores we report in the text and in Table 1. (Traditional stimulus accuracy scores are reported in the note to the table, for comparison.)

Table 1

Relationship Closeness:
Unbiased Hit Rate at Decoding Expressed and Concealed Emotions

	Happy	*Sad*	*Angry*
Expressiveness			
Express clearly			
Closer friends	66.6	66.3	66.9
Less close friends	75.0	56.3	49.5
Strangers	47.0	49.2	38.7
Conceal			
Closer friends	22.3	15.9	15.0
Less close friends	14.6	54.7	32.3
Strangers	21.9	21.8	21.1

Note. For the Emotion X Expressiveness X Closeness interaction, the mean square error was 6.00. The means listed in the table are unbiased hit rates. The mean percent accuracy scores (i.e., stimulus accuracy) for happy, sad, and angry respectively were 72.5, 68.8, and 68.1 for express clearly, closer friends. For express clearly, less close friends, (happy, sad, and angry, respectively), the mean percent accuracy scores were 75.0, 59.4, and 51.0. For express clearly, strangers, the mean percent accuracy scores were 54.3, 52.4, and 44.1. For conceal, closer friends, the mean percent accuracy scores were 31.3, 22.5, and 15.0. For conceal, less close friends, the mean percent accuracy scores were 17.7, 62.5, and 32.3. For conceal, strangers, the mean percent accuracy scores were 27.2, 24.9, and 27.3.

Was Accuracy Greater Than Chance?

An ANOVA was conducted in which the unbiased hit rate and the hit rate expected by chance were levels of a dependent variable. The actual unbiased hit rate was 38.5%, which was substantially greater than the unbiased hit rate expected by chance (7.9%), $F(1, 44) = 189.72, p < .0001$. In addition, all three emotions were read at levels that were substantially greater than chance. Unbiased hit rate for the happy stories was 39.4%, as compared to a rate expected by chance of 8.3%, $F(1, 88) = 84.63, p < .0001$. For the sad stories, the unbiased hit rate of 41.7% exceeded the chance level of 8.6%, $F(1, 88) = 93.84, p < .0001$. Similarly, the unbiased hit rate for the anger stories, 34.4%, was greater than the chance level of 6.7%, $F(1, 88) = 67.92, p < .0001$. Stories for which the emotion was expressed clearly were substantially easier to read ($M = 54.5\%$) than stories for which the emotion was concealed ($M = 22.5\%$), $F(1, 44) = 144.45, p < .0001$. However, even stories for which the emotion was concealed were read at a level substantially greater than what would be expected by chance (6.7%), $F(1, 44) = 18.525, p < .0001$.

Differences between Friends and Strangers

Across all of the stories (expressed and concealed), judges were significantly more accurate at determining the emotional content of the stories when the senders were their friends ($M = 43.7\%$) than when they were strangers ($M = 33.3\%$), $F(1, 44) = 7.47, p = .01$. The results of a nearly significant interaction between the sender-judge relationship and the expressiveness of the senders' stories, $F(1, 44) = 3.43, p = .07$, supported our prediction that friends would be better than strangers at reading emotions that were expressed clearly (64.0% versus 45.0%); friends were not more accurate than strangers at reading concealed emotions (23.5% versus 21.6%). A direct comparison of friends to strangers for the emotions that were expressed clearly was significant, $F(1, 44) = 10.09, p = .003$.

Our prediction that friends and strangers would differ in their accuracy at reading concealed negative emotions would have been supported by a three-way interaction of relationship, expressiveness, and emotional content. However, this effect was not significant, $F(2, 88) = 1.13, p = .33$.

Sex Differences

As predicted, judges were more accurate at guessing the emotional content of female senders' stories ($M = 42.7\%$) than male senders' stories ($M = 34.3\%$), $F(1, 44) = 4.64, p = .04$. However, there were no indications that this effect reversed for expressions of anger; for the interaction of sender sex and emotional content, $F(2, 88) = .03, p = .97$. There were also no significant differences in the accuracy scores of male and female judges, $F(1, 44) = 0.21, p = .65$. The interaction of judge sex and emotional content was also nonsignificant, $F(2, 88) = 2.42, p = .09$,

34

and the direction of the effect was opposite to predictions, in that it was the women, and not the men, who tended to identify anger more accurately ($M = 40.1\%$ for women vs. 28.7% for men). Based on the accommodatingness hypothesis (Rosenthal & DePaulo, 1979), we predicted that women would be more accurate than men at reading the clearly expressed emotions but not the concealed ones. The means were in the predicted direction, but the interaction of judge sex with expressiveness was not significant, $F(1, 44) = 1.94, p = .17$.

Friendship Closeness

Our prediction that friends would differ from strangers in reading concealed cues to negativity was not supported. However, using the relationship closeness data we collected, we were able to examine whether closer friends might differ from less close friends in their reading of those cues. The relationship closeness measure that we collected, the Relationship Closeness Inventory (Berscheid et al., 1989) is based on an interdependence construal of closeness. Close partners are those who interact frequently, who share a variety of activities, and who influence each other's plans and goals. We computed the mean of the RCI scores for each friendship pair. These mean RCI scores could range from 0 to 30, and the median score was 11. Each pair of friends was categorized as closer or less close according to a median split. The mean RCI score for close friends was 14.8; for the less close friends, it was 8.36.

In our original design, relationship status was a repeated measures factor: Each judge rated a friend and a stranger. However, our closeness factor was a between-participants factor: Each judge was either "closer" or "less close" to his or her friend. Therefore, it was not possible to include strangers, closer friends, and less close friends in the same analysis. Only the closer and less close friends were included. All other factors were the same as those used in the previous analysis.

There was no overall difference in accuracy between closer friends and less close friends, $F(1, 40) = 0.61, p = .44$. However, the three-way interaction (Emotion x Expressiveness x Closeness) was significant, $F(2, 80) = 4.29, p = .02$. Closer friends were non-significantly better than less close friends at reading clearly expressed sadness and anger, $F(1, 80) = 2.06, p = .16$. (Contrast weights were +1 for sadness and anger for the closer friends, and -1 for sadness and anger for the less close friends.) However, closer friends were markedly worse than less close friends at recognizing *disguised* sadness and anger, $F(1, 80) = 8.63, p = .004$. (Contrast weights were -1 for disguised sadness and anger for the closer friends and +1 for the less close friends.) In fact, the closer friends tended to do slightly worse than even the strangers at reading disguised negativity. Closer and less close friends did not differ in their accuracy at reading clearly expressed happiness, $F(1, 80) = 0.39, p = .53$, or concealed happiness, $F(1, 80) = 0.35, p = .55$. Table 1 shows the unbiased hit rates for this interaction, and also includes the unbiased hit rates of the strangers, for comparison. (Traditional "stimulus accuracy" scores are reported in the note to the table.)

35

Although closer friends were superior to all other judges at reading sadness and anger when those emotions were expressed clearly, that advantage disappeared when those negative emotions were deliberately concealed. Closer friends were markedly worse than less close friends at recognizing disguised sadness and anger; in fact, the closer friends even tended to do slightly worse than the strangers at reading disguised negativity.

Except for the main effect of expressiveness (showing, of course, that the clearly expressed emotions were read more accurately than the concealed ones, $F(1, 40) = 32.32, p < .001$), no other effects were significant.

Discussion

What are the advantages of relationship closeness in the reading of nonverbal cues to emotions? In the non-problematic situation in which the experienced emotion is positive and non-threatening (i.e., happiness) and the person experiencing it is trying to express it clearly, closeness is linked to greater understanding. Clear expressions of happiness are more accurately identified by people's friends than by strangers. So, too, are clear expressions of sadness and anger.

However, when people deliberately try to conceal their emotions, their friends are no more accurate than strangers at recognizing those hidden feelings. If we had not looked beyond this comparison between the strangers and all of the friends, there would be no need to posit a motivational mechanism for the findings. There is no puzzle to the question of why concealed emotions are more difficult to read than clearly expressed ones. If the concealed negative emotions were more difficult to read than the concealed positive emotion, or (especially) if they were more difficult for the friends than for the strangers, then a simple explanation based on the clarity of the cues would be less tenable. But in the analysis in which all friends were considered together, this did not occur. The specific content of the emotion did not moderate any of the effects. This was not a simple matter of insufficient statistical power. The direction of the effect was not in line with the pattern we just described. When all of the friends were considered together (as they were in the initial analysis), the friends were nonsignificantly better than strangers at reading the concealed negative emotions.

On the basis of that analysis alone, then, our most parsimonious explanation would have been that all of the concealed emotions were equally indecipherable to all of the judges, probably because of the actual ambiguity of the cues. And in fact, in our interpretation of the difficulty that the strangers had in reading concealed emotions, we think that the objective nature of the stimuli may be a sufficient explanation. The strangers' accuracy at reading the concealed negative emotions was almost identical to their accuracy at reading concealed happiness.

It is important, though, that the concealed emotions were not completely indecipherable. Overall, accuracy at reading the concealed emotions was greater than chance. Even more importantly, when we looked separately at friends who were especially close to each other, compared to those

36

who were less close, it became evident that the inscrutability of the cues depended importantly on the closeness of the friendship and the negativity of the emotional content.

Liabilities of Closeness in Reading Nonverbal Cues

Strikingly, it was the closer friends who were especially inept at identifying concealed negativity. They even tended to be a shade worse than strangers at seeing the disguised sadness and anger. It was the less close friends who were especially skillful at the very difficult task of reading negative emotions that others are trying to conceal, with only nonverbal cues available to inform their judgments.

According the motivated inaccuracy model of Ickes and Simpson (1997), accuracy should be lowest when a relationship partner has thoughts or feelings that could prove distressing to the perceiver, and those sentiments are not clearly expressed. In the condition in which senders were trying to conceal their emotions, all of the judges, whether closer friends, less close friends, or strangers, were faced with ambiguous signals. But the three groups of judges were not equivalent in their potential to be threatened by the accurate recognition of negativity. The closer friends, whose lives were more interdependent than those of the less close friendship pairs, had more to lose than the less close friends (or, of course, the strangers) by accurately perceiving concealed negativity (Whitesell & Harter, 1996).

All of the judges knew that the senders were describing experiences from their lives that made them feel very happy, very sad, or very angry, but they knew nothing about the source of those emotions. Moreover, they could only see the senders, and could not hear any of their words. The concern that the senders may have been describing something the judge did that made them feel angry or sad, or something about the relationship that they found distressing, could be experienced only by the judges who were friends with the senders. Of those friends, the closer ones may have felt more threatened by that possibility. Therefore, their inaccuracy (relative to the less close friends) at reading the concealed negative emotions but not the concealed positive one, may have been motivated. In contrast, the less close friends shared the advantage potentially available to the closer friends of practice and experience at reading the emotions of their relationship partners, without feeling as reluctant to notice negativity. In fact, if the less close friends had become less close over time, perhaps as a result of tensions and disagreements, they may have been especially motivated to see negativity, which they might regard as evidence for their suspicions that beneath their partner's false display of friendliness and cheer is at least some degree of anger or malcontent. Of course, this is merely one possible explanation for less close friends' accuracy at decoding concealed negative emotions. Longitudinal work will be needed to address this possibility, as well as alternatives based on different assumptions about the direction of causality (e.g., perhaps sensitivity to hidden negative emotions undermines relationship closeness). Specifically, hierarchical linear modeling could be used to test the effect of changes in relationship closeness over time on accuracy at decoding nonverbal cues to emotion.

An alternative to the motivated inaccuracy explanation is that the judges were motivated not by feelings of threat to themselves or their relationship (if any) with the senders but by concern for senders. In overlooking just those emotions that the senders were trying to hide, they may have been politely affording the senders a zone of emotional privacy (DePaulo, Wetzel, Sternglanz, & Walker Wilson, 2003; Rosenthal & DePaulo, 1979). When we first introduced this hypothesis, we suggested that relationship partners may be less willing to maintain an emotional distance from their friends' concealed feelings. Members of close relationships may try to discern hidden feelings because they care about how their partners really are feeling, or because they believe that emotions should be shared rather than cloaked. From this perspective, it should have been the closer friends, rather than the less close friends, who were better at identifying concealed emotions. But, of course, the reverse was true, and only for the concealed negative emotions. An alternative possibility is that partners who allow each other room to keep some of their emotions to themselves, particularly their negative emotions, find that their relationships are consequently strengthened rather than undermined. These possibilities are admittedly speculative, and in need of further research. A longitudinal study of platonic friends would be useful to determine whether the act of allowing "emotional space" predicts subsequent relationship closeness.

There is one other interpretation that we see as potentially important. It starts with the acknowledgment that in the context of relationships (though not only in those contexts), emotions are not just there to be interpreted or shared; rather, they are often calls to action. Clark and her colleagues have made a compelling case for this position as it applies to the expression of emotions (Clark, Fitness, & Brissette, 2000). They argue, for example, that a person will express emotions more often and more clearly to those who are likely to feel more responsible for that person's needs. Our own interest is in the people perceiving the emotion cues. If they feel more responsible for the needs of the sender, should they be more skillful at reading the sender's emotions, including even the hidden negative ones? We think that the answer will depend on whether the perceiver wants to attend to those needs. For example, Clark and her colleagues note that when people are eager to form new relationships, they like potential partners better when they seem to be experiencing emotions, including even negative ones, than when they seem to be in an emotionally neutral mood. From our perspective, the perceivers in those situations hope to act on the calls for help that expressions of emotions can convey, and that desire will enhance their nonverbal sensitivity (cf. DePaulo, Brittingham, & Kaiser, 1983). In the context of relationships that are already established, it is the closer partners who are likely to feel more responsible for each other's needs. But that felt obligation can motivate them to miss or misinterpret cues of sadness or anger if they are hoping not to have to provide comfort to a sad friend or deal with the wrath of an angry one. They may also prefer not to notice such cues if they believe that their partner is unconsolable (cf. Simpson, Ickes, & Blackstone, 1995). In cases in which the distress or anger is aimed at them, inaccuracy can be motivated by the fear that it would be too difficult to resist the temptation to reciprocate the hostilities (e.g., Rusbult et al., 1986, 1991). For less close friends, it may be easier to notice hidden cues to sadness or anger (which they may be especially skilled at doing, because of their experiences in the relationship) and then simply ignore them. As an explanation for the results of the present research, we find the interpretation of emotions as calls to action less convincing than the explanation suggesting

38

that the closer friends' inaccuracy was motivated by threat (i.e., the Ickes & Simpson, 1997, model). However, we do think that the obligations for action that emotions convey, particularly in relationship contexts, is a topic that merits more attention.

Future Directions

We expected perceivers' relationship status as friends or strangers with the senders would be one of the most important predictors of their accuracy. But this crude distinction provided only crude conclusions: The friends were generally better than the strangers at reading nonverbal cues to emotions. The more illuminating findings followed from a distinction between the friends who were very close to each other and those who were less close. A similar pattern was recently reported in a longitudinal study of deception detection between same-sex friends (Anderson et al., 2002). When all of the friends were considered together, they showed no advantage at all in their ability to detect each other's lies. However, when the closer friends were compared to the friends who were less close, the closer friends, but not the less close ones, did learn to detect each other's deception more successfully over time. Future studies of interpersonal sensitivity between friends are likely to benefit from the systematic recruitment of friendship pairs who differ in closeness.

In the literature on relationships, studies of romantic relationships have been primarily studies of opposite sex pairs, whereas studies of platonic friendships have typically been studies of same-sex pairs. We thought it was important to go beyond the standard paradigm, especially because of the hints in the literature that sex differences could be especially important in the nonverbal communication of anger. Notably, we found no evidence whatsoever that friendship effects were qualified by gender composition; patterns of nonverbal sensitivity and insensitivity were the same for same-sex friends as they were for opposite-sex friends. Still, we are not ready to rule out the possibility that gender composition could matter in other kinds of communications between friends. Future research would benefit from focus on these non-standard pairings, as well as other pairings such as parent-child and older adult intimates.

Anger also turned out not to be the special case that we had expected. Men's expressions of anger were no more clearly read than were women's, nor were men any more accurate at reading other people's anger. This cannot be straightforwardly attributed to the inclusion of friends in our study, which set it apart from most previous studies involving strangers. We found no indications even among the strangers in our study that men communicated anger more successfully than the women. One way our study did differ from other studies of anger in the literature is that all participants came to the study with a friend. Although the senders were separated from their friend when they were describing their emotional experiences, it is possible that they had their friends in mind as they told their stories, and their nonverbal expressions were therefore similar to their usual expressions in their face-to-face communications with their friends (Fridlund, 1991). Expressions of emotions communicated with a particular relationship partner in mind may be different from displays produced outside of a relationship context (Buck et al., 1992; Wagner &

Smith, 1991), which may be more akin to displays of dominance. These ideas are, of course, speculative and tentative; what is more certain is the need for further study of the communication of emotions between friends.

Conclusions

Our findings suggest that especially close friends may be motivated to misperceive each others' concealed negative emotions. Friends who are not so close are more accurate at identifying those suppressed cues to negativity. Perhaps people interpret their friends' hidden negative cues most accurately when they are having problems in their relationship, or when they are angry at each other; for it is only in these acrimonious situations that friends will have the advantages of familiarity without the usual liabilities of seeing each other through rose-colored glasses.

References

Anderson, D. E. (1999). Cognitive and motivational processes underlying truth bias. Unpublished doctoral dissertation, University of Virginia.

Anderson, D. E., Ansfield, M. E., & DePaulo, B. M. (1999). Love's best habit: Deception in the context of relationships. In P. Philippot, R. S. Feldman, & E. J. Coats (Eds.), *The social context of nonverbal behavior* (pp. 372-409). Cambridge: Cambridge University Press.

Anderson, D. E., DePaulo, B. M., & Ansfield, M. E. (2002). The development of deception detection skill: A longitudinal study of same sex friends. *Personality and Social Psychology Bulletin, 28*, 536-545.

Ansfield, M. E., DePaulo, B. M., & Bell, K. L. (1995). Familiarity effects in nonverbal understanding: Recognizing our own facial expressions and our friends'. *Journal of Nonverbal Behavior, 19*, 135-149.

Berscheid, E., Snyder, M., & Omoto, A. M. (1989). The Relationship Closeness Inventory: Assessing the closeness of interpersonal relationships. *Journal of Personality and Social Psychology, 57*, 792-807.

Bonebright, T. L., Thompson, J. L., & Leger, D. W. (1996). Gender stereotypes in the expression and perception of vocal affect. *Sex Roles, 34*, 429-445.

Buck, R., Losow, J. I., Murphy, M. M., & Costanzo, P. (1992). Social facilitation and inhibition of emotion expression and communication. *Journal of Personality and Social Psychology, 63,* 962-968.

Clark, M. S., Fitness, J., & Brissette, I. (2000). Understanding people's perceptions of relationships is crucial to understanding their emotional lives. In G. Fletcher & M. S. Clark (Eds.), *Blackwood handbook of social psychology: Interpersonal processes* (pp. 253-278). London: Blackwell.

Coats, E. J., & Feldman, R. S. (1996). Gender differences in nonverbal correlates of social status. *Personality and Social Psychology Bulletin, 22*, 1014-1022.

DePaulo, B. M. (1992). Nonverbal behavior and self-presentation. *Psychological Bulletin, 111*, 203-243.

DePaulo, B. M., Brittingham, G. L., & Kaiser, M. K. (1983). Receiving competence-relevant help: Effects on reciprocity, affect, and sensitivity to the helper's nonverbally expressed needs. *Journal of Personality and Social Psychology, 45*, 1045-1060.

DePaulo, B. M., & Kashy, D. A. (1998). Everyday lies in close and casual relationships. *Journal of Personality and Social Psychology, 74*, 63-79.

DePaulo, B. M., Wetzel, C., Sternglanz, R. W., & Walker Wilson, M. W. (2003). Verbal and nonverbal dynamics of privacy, secrecy, and deceit. *Journal of Social Issues, 59*, 391-410.

De Waal, F. (1996). *Good natured: The origins of right and wrong in humans and other animals*. Cambridge: Harvard University Press.

Fleming, J. H., Darley, J. M., Hilton, J. L., & Kojetin, B. A. (1990). Multiple audience problem: A strategic communication perspective on social perception. *Journal of Personality and Social Psychology, 58*, 593-609.

Fridlund, A. J. (1991). Sociality of solitary smiling: Potentiation by an implicit audience. *Journal of Personality and Social Psychology, 60*, 229-240.

Gottman, J. M. (1979). *Marital interaction: Experimental investigations*. New York: Academic Press.

Hall, J. A. (1984). *Nonverbal sex differences: Communication accuracy and expressive style*. Baltimore, MD: Johns Hopkins University Press.

Hall, J. A. (1987). On explaining gender differences: The case of nonverbal communication. In P. Shaver & C. Hendrick (Eds.), *Review of Personality and Social Psychology* (Vol. 7, pp. 177-200). Newbury Park, CA: Sage.

Hodgins, H. S., & Zuckerman, M. (1990). The effect of nonverbal sensitivity on social interaction. *Journal of Nonverbal Behavior, 14*, 155-170.

Ickes, W., & Simpson, J. A. (1997). Managing empathic accuracy in close relationships. In W. Ickes (Ed.), *Empathic accuracy* (pp. 218-250). New York: Guilford Press.

Knudson, R. M., Sommers, A. A., & Golding, S. L. (1980). Interpersonal perception and mode of resolution in marital conflict. *Journal of Personality and Social Psychology, 38*, 751-763.

Murray, S. L., & Holmes, J. G. (1999). The (mental) ties that bind: Cognitive structures that predict relationship resilience. *Journal of Personality and Social Psychology, 77*, 1228-1244.

Murray, S. L., Holmes, J. G., & Griffin, D. W. (1996). The benefits of positive illusions: Idealization and the construction of satisfaction in close relationships. *Journal of Personality and Social Psychology, 70*, 79-98.

Noller, P., & Ruzzene, M. (1991). Communication in marriage: The influence of affect and cognition. In G. J. O. Fletcher & F. D. Fincham (Eds.), *Cognition in close relationships* (pp. 203-233). Hillsdale, NJ: Erlbaum.

Rosenthal, R., & DePaulo, B. M. (1979). Sex differences in eavesdropping on nonverbal cues. *Journal of Personality and Social Psychology, 37*, 273-285.

Rosenthal, R., & Rosnow, R. L. (1991). *Essentials of behavioral research* (2nd ed.). New York: McGraw-Hill.

Rotter, N. G., & Rotter, G. S. (1988). Sex differences in the encoding and decoding of negative facial emotions. *Journal of Nonverbal Behavior, 12*, 139-148.

Rusbult, C. E., Johnson, D. J., & Morrow, G. D. (1986). Determinants and consequences of exit, voice, loyalty, and neglect: Responses to dissatisfaction in adult romantic involvements. *Human Relations, 39*, 45-63.

Rusbult, C. E., Verette, J., Whitney, G. A., Slovik, L. F., & Lipkus, I. (1991). Accommodation processes in close relationships: Theory and preliminary evidence. *Journal of Personality and Social Psychology, 60*, 53-78.

Sabatelli, R. M., Buck, R., & Dreyer, A. (1982). Nonverbal communication accuracy in married couples: Relationship with marital complaints. *Journal of Personality and Social Psychology, 43*, 1088-1097.

41

Sabatelli, R. M., Dreyer, A., & Buck, R. (1979). Cognitive style and the sending and receiving of facial cues. *Perceptual and Motor Skills, 49*, 203-212.

Schlenker, B. R., & Britt, T. W. (2001). Strategically controlling information to help friends: Effects of empathy and friendship strength on beneficial impression management. *Journal of Experimental Social Psychology, 37*, 357-372.

Sillars, A. L. (1985). Interpersonal perception in relationships. In W. Ickes (Ed.), *Compatible and incompatible relationships* (pp. 277-305). New York: Springer-Verlag.

Sillars, A. L., Pike, G. R., Jones, T. S., & Murphy, M. A. (1984). Communication and understanding in marriage. *Human Communication Research, 10*, 317-350.

Simpson, J. A., Ickes, W., & Blackstone, T. (1995). When the head protects the heart: Empathic accuracy in dating relationships. *Journal of Personality and Social Psychology, 69*, 629-641.

Snedecor, J. C., & Cochran, W. G. (1967). *Statistical methods* (6th ed.). Ames, Iowa: Iowa State University Press.

Stinson, L., & Ickes, W. (1992). Empathic accuracy in the interactions of male friends versus male strangers. *Journal of Personality and Social Psychology, 62*, 787-797.

Tavris, C. (1982). *Anger: The misunderstood emotion.* New York: Simon & Schuster.

Tice, D. M., Butler, J. L., Muraven, M. B., & Stillwell, A. M. (1995). When modesty prevails: Differential favorability of self-presentation to friends and strangers. *Journal of Personality and Social Psychology, 69*, 1120-1138.

Wagner, H. L. (1993). On measuring performance in category judgment studies of nonverbal behavior. *Journal of Nonverbal Behavior, 17*, 3-28.

Wagner, H. L., MacDonald, C. J., & Manstead, A. S. R. (1986). Communication of individual emotions by spontaneous facial expressions. *Journal of Personality and Social Psychology, 50*, 737-743.

Wagner, H. L., & Smith, J. (1991). Facial expression in the presence of friends and strangers. *Journal of Nonverbal Behavior, 15*, 201-214.

Whitesell, N. R., & Harter, S. (1996). The interpersonal context of emotion: Anger with close friends and classmates. *Child Development, 67*, 1345-1359.

Winer, B. J. (1971). *Statistical principles in experimental design* (2nd ed.). New York: McGraw-Hill.

Zuckerman, M., & Przewuzman, S. J. (1979). Decoding and encoding facial expressions in preschool age children. *Environmental Psychology and Nonverbal Behavior, 3*, 147-163.

Author Notes

This study was supported in part by a grant from NSF to the second author. Portions of this research were presented at the June 2000 conference of the American Psychological Society in Miami Beach, Florida, and the February 2001 conference of the Society for Personality and Social Psychology in San Antonio, Texas. We wish to thank William Ickes and two anonymous reviewers for their thoughtful comments on earlier drafts of this manuscript. We also wish to thank Rachel Bradburn, Autumn Dickman, Chris Hanson, Kate Lyng, Kate Nuckols, Brandon Phillips, Thomas Ramsson, Amanda Shaver, and Lena Tashjian for their assistance in conducting this research.

Footnote

[1] This technique of yoking each dyad with a stranger from the last session was employed to ensure that each sender was judged precisely once by both a friend and a stranger. This was indeed the case for most senders; however, eight judges coincidentally knew the sender who was supposed to be their "stranger"; in these eight cases, judges viewed a tape of a different sender (who was truly a stranger to the judge). Thus, eight senders were judged twice by a stranger, while another eight senders were not judged at all by a stranger.

Journal of Personality and Social Psychology, 1998, *74*, 63-79.

Everyday Lies in Close and Casual Relationships

Bella M. DePaulo and Deborah A. Kashy

In 2 diary studies, 77 undergraduates and 70 community members recorded their social interactions and lies for a week. Because lying violates the openness and authenticity that people value in their close relationships, we predicted (and found) that participants would tell fewer lies per social interaction to the people to whom they felt closer and would feel more uncomfortable when they did lie to those people. Because altruistic lies can communicate caring, we also predicted (and found) that relatively more of the lies told to best friends and friends would be altruistic than self-serving, whereas the reverse would be true of lies told to acquaintances and strangers. Also consistent with predictions, lies told to closer partners were more often discovered.

To understand the role of lying in close and casual relationships, it may be important to understand both the nature of the lies that are told in everyday life and the nature of close relationships. Over the past several decades, a handful of studies of lying in everyday life have been published (Camden, Motley, & Wilson, 1984 ; DePaulo, Kashy, Kirkendol, Wyer, & Epstein, 1996 ; Hample, 1980 ; Lippard, 1988 ; Metts, 1989 ; Turner, Edgley, & Olmstead, 1975), including most recently, the first such investigation to include a separate sample of adult participants who were not all college students (DePaulo et al., 1996). These studies have greatly increased our knowledge of the nature and frequency of lying in everyday life. They indicate that lying is a fact of daily life. In the DePaulo et al. (1996) studies, for example, in which lying was defined as "intentionally [trying] to mislead someone" (p. 981), the demographically diverse participants from the community reported telling an average of one lie in every five of their social interactions, and the college student participants reported telling a lie in every three interactions. In both groups, the participants were about twice as likely to tell lies that benefited themselves in some way (self-centered lies) than to tell lies that benefited others (other-oriented, or altruistic,

45

lies). Of the self-centered lies, some of them were told in the pursuit of material gain or personal convenience, but far more of them were told for psychological reasons. By their own accounts, people told their everyday lies to try to make themselves look better or feel better, to protect themselves from embarrassment or disapproval or from having their feelings hurt, and to try to gain the esteem and affection of other people. Although participants told many lies about their achievements and their failures, their actions, plans, and whereabouts, and the reasons for their actions or inactions, the lies that they told most often were about their feelings. When people told other-oriented lies, they often pretended to feel more positively than they really did feel, and they often claimed to agree with other people when in fact they disagreed. In short, in everyday life, people lie about what they are really like and how they really do feel.

Rates of Lying in Close and Casual Relationships

When people talk about what is special to them about their personal relationships and about what closeness means to them (Argyle & Henderson, 1984 ; Maxwell, 1985 ; Parks & Floyd, 1996), they underscore the importance of talking, disclosing, and confiding—of "telling each other everything" (Parks & Floyd, 1996, p. 94) and of trusting that their confidences will be kept. They also describe issues of authenticity, noting that they can show their true feelings and be themselves, with no need to try to impress the other person. Although these self-reports may be idealized, the literature does offer some support for them. For example, people are more self-enhancing with strangers than with friends (Tice, Butler, Muraven, & Stillwell, 1995). Also, the relationship qualities that people value predict important relational outcomes. For example, self-disclosure predicts marital satisfaction (Hendrick, 1981), and trusting and confiding are positively correlated with the quality and enduringness of friendships (Argyle & Henderson, 1984).

People's reports of what they value in their relationships also dovetail with important theoretical statements about the significance of personal relationships. For example, Deci and Ryan (1991) believe that there are three primary psychological needs, and one of them is the need for relatedness (see also Baumeister & Leary, 1995). This need "encompasses a person's strivings to relate to and care for others, [and] to feel that those others are relating authentically to one's self" (p. 243). Similarly, Reis and Patrick (1996) argued for the profound importance of intimacy to human well-being. They define intimacy as "an interactive process in which, as a result of a partner's response, individuals come to feel understood, validated, and cared for" (p. 536). From attachment theory comes the proposition that "humans possess basic needs that are naturally satisfied by social relationships" (Hazan & Shaver, 1994, p. 10), and that the most basic need is for felt security. Feelings of security, in turn, depend largely on the answer to the question "Can I trust my partner to be available and responsive to my needs?" (p. 13). Trustworthy partners, according to Holmes and Rempel (1989), are dependable people who can be counted on to be honest and benevolent.

None of these theoretical perspectives offers explicit predictions about the rates of everyday lying in close and casual relationships. However, the prediction that lying occurs at lower rates in closer relationships would probably be consistent with all of them. Lying is by definition an inauthentic communication; as such, it cannot serve the need for genuine relatedness. When people lie about who they really are and how they really feel, they cannot elicit understanding or validation of the person they really believe themselves to be. They also cannot easily serve as targets of secure attachment, because people who lie especially often to promote their own needs are unlikely to be trusted to be responsive to other people's needs.

We predicted, then, that people will lie less often in close relationships than in casual ones. Also, because lie telling violates close relationship ideals such as openness and authenticity, we predicted that when people do lie to their close relationship partners, they will feel more distressed than when they lie to partners in casual relationships (Miller, Mongeau, & Sleight, 1986). They will feel more uncomfortable as they anticipate telling the lie, as they actually tell it, and just after they have told it.

Kinds of Lies in Close and Casual Relationships

The theoretical perspectives we described underscore the significance of authenticity and trustworthiness in close personal relationships. But they also point to the importance of caring and emotional support. One way that people might try to communicate their love and concern for the important people in their lives is by telling altruistic lies. They compliment them, pretend to agree with them, and claim to understand. The meta-messages of these lies may be supportive rather than threatening (cf. Ruesch & Bateson, 1951 ; Watzlawick, Beavin, & Jackson, 1967). By lying, the liars may be saying that they care more about the other person's feelings than the truth.

Our initial prediction was that people will tell fewer lies to closer relationship partners. We added a second prediction: When people do lie to partners in close relationships, relatively more of the lies will be altruistic than self-centered.

Beyond Closeness: Other Predictors of Lying

In addition to the emotional considerations we have described, there may also be practical reasons for a lower rate of everyday lying in closer relationships than in more casual ones. For example, the possibilities for successful deception in close personal relationships may be constrained by the knowledge that the partners share about each other. A college student can try to convince a casual acquaintance that his father is an ambassador (as one of ours did), but the same lie will not succeed with a close friend who already knows that the "ambassador" is actually a bartender. Relationship partners who have known each other for a long time may be especially likely to have, or to be perceived as having, detailed knowledge about each other's lives that would discourage many attempts at deceit.

In some instances, partners do not already know the truth that a person might be tempted to cover with a lie. Even in those cases, however, people may fear that their partners are more likely to discover the truth eventually if they are close partners, who typically interact frequently (Nezlek, 1995), than if they are only casual relationship partners. People who interact with each other on a regular basis may be vulnerable to this fear of eventual detection even if they are not emotionally close to each other.

These arguments predict that people will less often attempt to lie to their close relationship partners, to people they have known for a long time, and to people with whom they interact frequently. It also follows that when lies are told to such people, those lies are more likely eventually to be discovered. Objective evidence will surface that will betray the deceits, or the liars will become entangled in their own webs of deceit as they struggle to keep their stories consistent.

People in close relationships may also fear that their lies are more likely to be immediately transparent to close relationship partners, who may have developed a special sensitivity to their nonverbal and verbal clues to deceit, than to casual partners (Anderson, Ansfield, & DePaulo, in press). Regardless of whether this fear is justified, it can act as a deterrent to lying to close relationship partners. When people do lie to close partners, they may be less likely to feel confident that their partners believed their lies. In the present research, we asked participants to indicate whether they thought each lie had been believed at the time that they told it. Then, a week or so later, we asked whether the lie had been discovered.

Relationship partners are not always seekers of the truth. As Ekman and Friesen (1969) pointed out several decades ago, people can collaborate to maintain rather than discover each other's lies. Partners in close relationships, more so than those in casual ones, come to know each other's sensitive and taboo topics (Baxter & Wilmot, 1985). By steering clear of such treacherous turf, they can reduce their partners' temptations to lie.

Other processes could also be important in predicting rates of lying in different relationships. For example, Millar and Tesser (1988) hypothesized that people lie when their behavior violates the expectations that another person holds for them. They found support for their predictions in role-play studies of parent–child and employee–employer relationships. The violated expectations model generates a prediction at odds with our own: Because close relationship partners hold more expectations about each other than do casual partners, the rate of lying in close relationships might be higher. On the other hand, the expectations we hold about close relationship partners may be more realistic than the expectations we hold for acquaintances and strangers, and therefore they may be less likely to be violated.

Varieties of Closeness

When the study of personal relationships was just beginning, closeness was often operationalized in terms of different relationship categories (Berscheid, Snyder, & Omoto, 1989a). Marriages and parent–child relationships, for example, were sometimes assumed to be "closer" relationships than friendships. These kinds of assumptions were later questioned, as it became apparent that particular relationships within categories vary greatly in closeness, and that relationship categories vary in many important ways other than closeness. For example, romantic relationships may be uniquely characterized by certain kinds of self-presentational concerns. Relationships that are asymmetrical in power, such as those between parents and children, may also differ importantly in deception-relevant ways from those that are more symmetrical. For instance, people who have less power may be tempted to lie to those who have more power in order to obtain the resources they control (cf. Hample, 1980 ; Lippard, 1988).

In the present research, participants identified each of their interaction partners as a stranger, acquaintance, friend, best friend, romantic partner, spouse, parent, child, sibling, or other relative. To test our hypothesis that fewer lies would be told to closer relationship partners, we first considered only those relationship categories that we believed to vary primarily in closeness: strangers, acquaintances, friends, and best friends. Thus, romantic partners, spouses, parents, and other family members were not included. Our prediction would be supported if participants lied most frequently to strangers, then acquaintances, and least frequently to best friends. Second, we used three measures of closeness (described below) that are independent of relationship type, and we examined the relationship between closeness and rate of lying in analyses that included all dyadic interaction partners. Third, we tested the same links between closeness and rate of lying within each of the major relationship categories (friends, family members, acquaintances and strangers, romantic partners). In this most stringent test of our hypothesis, closeness and rate of lying should have been inversely related within every major relationship category.

Relationship researchers often assess "subjective closeness," which is a person's subjective emotional experience of "feeling close" to someone. This is usually measured on scales that ask people directly how close they feel to each of their partners. We used such a measure in the present research.

Still another measure of closeness was derived theoretically from interdependence theory. Kelley et al. (1983) hypothesized that close relationships are characterized by frequent and diverse interactions that endure over time and in which the partners influence each other's behavior and values. Berscheid, Snyder, and Omoto (1989b) developed the Relationship Closeness Inventory (RCI) to measure the frequency, strength, and diversity components of interdependence, which they summed together to form their overall index of closeness (they considered the duration of the relationship separately). The RCI is a measure of "behaving close," which is distinguishable from the subjective measures of "feeling close" (Aron, Aron, & Smollan, 1992). We did not use the RCI because it had not yet been published when our data were collected. However, we did have access to information similar to that generated by the RCI frequency subscale in the form of the number of dyadic social interactions participants reported with each of their partners (using a version of the Rochester Interaction Record [RIR]; Wheeler & Nezlek, 1977). This measure is probably a more accurate measure of interaction frequency than the RCI frequency subscale, which is based on participants' retrospective estimates of the amount of time they spent alone with each partner over the past week (Reis & Wheeler, 1991).

To assess endurance over time, we included the standard measure of relationship duration (participants' reports of the number of months or years they had known each partner). Thus, the present study measured three relationship qualities (subjective closeness, frequency of interaction, and relationship duration) as well as relationship type (e.g., friend, spouse).

We thought that all three operationalizations of closeness would predict rates of lying: People would lie less often to those relationship partners to whom they feel especially close, to those with whom they interact more frequently, and to those whom they have known for a longer time. However, because we believed that it is the emotional quality of close relationships that most strongly deters lying, we predicted that subjective emotional closeness would be the most important predictor. When the predictive power of all three types of closeness were tested together (by entering them into a simultaneous regression equation), only subjective closeness would remain a significant (negative) predictor of lying.

The Present Research

Our data are from two diary studies of lying in everyday life that were first described by DePaulo et al. (1996) and Kashy and DePaulo (1996) . DePaulo et al. (1996) presented a profile of everyday lying (e.g., the types of lies that were told, the reasons for lying, gender differences in lying), and Kashy and DePaulo (1996) reported personality predictors of lying in everyday life. The present report represents a unique contribution in its focus on everyday lying in different kinds of relationships.

In the two studies, 77 college students and 70 people from the community recorded all of their social interactions and all of the lies that they told during those social interactions every day for a week. Participants described each lie and the reason for telling it in their own words, and they also rated the characteristics of their lie-telling experiences (such as how distressed they felt while telling it and whether they thought it was believed). At the end of the week, they described the nature and closeness of their relationship with each of the persons with whom they had interacted, and they indicated for each lie whether or not it had been discovered.

The present research builds on previous research on lying in relationships in several important ways. First, it is more comprehensive than previous studies in which participants selected just one particular lie (Hample, 1980) or conversation (Turner et al., 1975) or situation (Metts, 1989) to describe. Second, it is the only research to include a measure of participants' opportunities to lie, that is, the number of social interactions they had with each partner. Previous studies that reported that people told more lies to close relationship partners than to casual ones (Hample, 1980 ; Lippard, 1988) are difficult to interpret, in that people interact more frequently with close partners than with casual ones (Nezlek, 1995). Rate of lying (number of lies per number of social interactions) is a more appropriate measure. Third, the community member sample described in this report (and in DePaulo et al., 1996, and Kashy & DePaulo, 1996) is the only group we know of in the literature on lying in everyday life that is not a group consisting solely of college students.1 Finally, the present research is especially comprehensive in the number of ways that relationships are assessed. Relationship type was documented, and patterns of lying were compared across the different types. Closeness was operationalized in three ways: as subjective closeness, frequency of interacting, and relationship longevity. We examined the links with lying of all three operationalizations of closeness in analyses that included all relationship partners; we also looked at the same links within major relationship categories, such as family and friends.

Method

Participants

Participants in Study 1 were 30 male and 47 female undergraduates who participated in partial fulfillment of a requirement for an introductory psychology course. They ranged in age from 17 to 22 (M = 18.69, SD = 0.91). Sixty-four were White, 9 were Black, and 4 described themselves as "other" than White or Black. The 77 participants do not include one man who completed only 2 days of the 7-day record keeping.

Participants in Study 2 were 30 men and 40 women who were recruited by means of advertisements posted at a local community college, from lists of people who had taken continuing education courses, and from lists of names selected randomly from the area telephone directory. They ranged in age from 18 to 71 (M = 34.19, SD = 12.49). Sixty-seven were White and 3 were Black. Other demographic information is based on 53 of the 70 participants, as 17 were inadvertently given the undergraduate demographic questionnaire, which included no questions about employment, education, marital status, or children. Of those who did answer the more extended questionnaire, 81% were employed, 57% were married, 47% had children, and 34% had no more than a high school education. The 70 participants in Study 2 do not include one man who said that he had recorded only about 10% of his social interactions and 5% of his lies.

Procedure

There were three phases to the study: an initial introductory session, the 7-day recording period, and a final phase during which participants answered additional questions about their lies and their experiences in the study.

Phase 1: Introduction to the study

The Study 1 participants and the participants from Study 2 who were recruited from the community college initially had responded to notices posted on a bulletin board in an academic building describing the research. The study was described as one in which they would keep records of their social interactions and communications for 7 days. In Study 1, the notice indicated that participants would receive partial course credit for their participation, and in Study 2, the notice indicated that participants would be paid $35. Study 2 participants recruited from continuing education lists or from the phone directory were sent letters with the same description of the research; then they were contacted by telephone about a week later.

All participants attended an initial 90-min meeting in which the study and the procedures were explained. In Study 1, these were group sessions attended by 10–15 participants at a time. The Study 2 sessions were conducted individually or in small groups.

Participants were told that they would be recording all of their social interactions and all of the lies that they told during those interactions every day for a week. It was noted that their role in this research was especially important in that they would be the observers and recorders of their own behavior. The investigators explained that they did not condone or condemn lying; rather, they were studying it scientifically and trying to learn the answers to some of the most fundamental questions about the phenomenon. They encouraged the participants to think of the study as an unusual opportunity to learn more about themselves.

The key terms were then explained to the participants. A "social interaction" was defined as "any exchange between you and another person that lasts 10 minutes or more . . . in which the behavior of one person is in response to the behavior of another person." This definition, plus many of the examples used to clarify the definition, were taken or adapted from the ones used in the initial studies involving the RIR (for example, Wheeler & Nezlek, 1977). We added an exception to the 10-min rule, which was that for any interaction in which participants told a lie, they were also to fill out a social interaction record, even if the interaction lasted less than 10 min. (For the college students and community members respectively, 8.9% and 10.5% of their lies were told during interactions lasting 10 min or less.) Copies of our adaptation of the RIR (see description below) were then distributed, and participants were told how to complete the form.

To explain what participants should count as a lie, we noted that "a lie occurs any time you intentionally try to mislead someone. Both the intent to deceive and the actual deception must occur." Many examples were given. Participants were urged to record all lies, no matter how big or how small. They were instructed that if they were uncertain as to whether a particular communication qualified as a lie, they should record it. (At the end of the study, two coders independently read through all of the lie diaries and agreed on the few that did not meet the definition and were therefore excluded.) The definition that we gave participants was interpreted broadly as encompassing any intentional attempts to mislead, including even nonverbal ones. The only example of a lie they were asked not to record was saying "fine" in response to perfunctory "How are you?" questions. Participants completed one deception record for every lie that they told. Sample records (see description below) were distributed, and the investigators explained how they were to be completed.

Participants were instructed to fill out the forms (social interaction records and deception records) at least once a day; it was suggested that they set aside a particular time or set of times to do so. During the week-long data collection period, the forms were collected by the experimenters at several different times. Participants were also given pocket-sized notebooks and were urged to carry them at all times. They were encouraged to use these notebooks to write down reminders of their social interactions and their lies as soon as possible after the events had taken place. Then

52

they could use their notes as an aid to their memory if they did not complete their social interaction and deception records until later in the day. The notebooks were not collected.

Several additional steps were taken to encourage the reporting of all lies. First, participants were told that if they did not wish to reveal the contents of any of the lies that they told, then in the space on the deception record in which they were to describe their lie, they could instead write "rather not say." That way, we, as investigators, would still know that a lie was told, and we would know other information about the lie and the social interaction in which it was told (from the other parts of the records that the participants completed). The content of 11 of the lies in the college student sample and none of the lies in the community sample were described as "rather not say." Second, we instructed participants that if they did not completely remember everything about a lie that they told, they should still fill out as much of the information on the form as they could. Third, we told participants that if they remembered a lie from a previous day that they had not recorded, they should still turn in a form for that lie.

The importance of accuracy and conscientiousness in keeping the records was emphasized throughout the session. To assure anonymity, we allowed participants to choose their own identification number, which they used throughout the study. Participants did not write their names on any of the forms.

At the end of the session, the investigators reviewed the amount of time it would take to complete all phases of the study and encouraged participants to terminate their participation at that point if they no longer had the interest or the time to participate fully. They were offered credit or payment even if they chose not to continue. All participants elected to continue.

Before they left, participants were given typed copies of all of the instructions and definitions they had been given during the session. This instruction booklet also included names and phone numbers of members of the research team with whom they had met and whom they could contact at any time with any questions or concerns they might have. Appointments were made with each participant to meet with a researcher in approximately 3 days to drop off completed social interaction forms and check on any questions related to the study. Researchers were available to collect forms at other times as well. Appointments were also made with all of the Study 1 participants to return once more at the end of the 7-day recording period to complete a final set of measures. Study 2 participants were shown an envelope and instructions that would be mailed to them at the end of the study so that they could complete the same measures.

Phase 2: Recording social interactions and lies

During the 7-day recording period, which began the day after the introductory session, participants completed a social interaction record for all of their social interactions and a deception record for all of their lies.

The social interaction record was adapted from the RIR (Wheeler & Nezlek, 1977). On each record, participants wrote their identification number and the date, time, and duration of the interaction. For interactions involving three or fewer other people, participants recorded the initials and the gender of each of those persons. (They kept a list of the initials of each of their interaction partners in the small notebooks that we gave them so that they could remember the initials and use the same ones for any given person each time.) For interactions with more than three other people, participants simply recorded the total number of male and female interaction partners. Participants then completed several scales describing the quality of the interaction. (These social interaction variables, described in DePaulo et al., 1996, are not relevant to the present report.)

Printed on the same page as the social interaction record was the deception record. Participants again indicated the initials and gender of the person(s) to whom they told their lie if there were three targets of the lie or fewer, or the number of males and number of females if there were more than three targets. (This information was the same as for the social interaction record except when participants directed their lie to a subset of the people involved in the interaction.) Below this was a blank space for participants to "briefly describe the lie" and another blank space for them to "briefly describe the reason why you told the lie." Next were nine 9-point rating scales. Participants rated their degree of planning of the lie on a scale with endpoints labeled completely spontaneous (1) and carefully planned in advance (9). Then they indicated the importance of not getting caught, from very unimportant (1) to very important (9). On the next three scales, they reported their feelings before the lie was told, while telling the lie, and after the lie was told, on a scale with endpoints labeled very comfortable (1) and very uncomfortable (9). They also rated the seriousness of the lie: very trivial, unimportant lie (1), to very serious, important lie (9); and the target's reaction to the lie: didn't believe me at all (1), to believed me completely (9). Finally, they answered two questions—"How would the target have felt if you told the truth instead of the lie?" and "How would you have felt if you told the truth instead of a lie?"—on scales with endpoints labeled much better if I told the truth (1) and much worse if I told the truth (9). The three ratings of comfort and the measure of the target's belief are of primary importance to the present report.[2]

Phase 3: Additional measures

After the completion of the 7-day recording period, participants were asked to respond to one more set of measures. First, we gave them a list of all of the initials they had used to refer to all of their interaction partners, and we asked them to fill out a separate form for each of those persons. On the forms, participants indicated the person's age and gender. Then they completed several 15-point scales. The ones relevant to this report were responses to the questions "How close do you feel to this person?" and "How much do you like this person?" Participants' responses to those two questions were highly correlated (college: $r = .84$, $p < .001$; community: $r = .81$, $p < .001$), and so they were averaged to form our measure of closeness. Participants also indicated how long they had known the person, in years, months, and days. This was our measure of the duration of the relationship. Because the data were highly skewed, we used a square root transformation of the total number of months in our analyses. Finally, participants checked off the particular category that best described their relationship with the person (best friend, friend, acquaintance, stranger, parent or guardian, spouse, child, brother or sister, other relative), and they indicated whether the relationship was romantic or not romantic.

Next, participants were given photocopies of each of the deception records they had completed. They answered two questions about each lie: "Was this lie ever discovered?" (participants checked one answer: no, not yet; don't know; or yes) and "If you could relive this social interaction, would you tell the lie again?" (participants checked either no or yes). The results of the first question are described in this report. Participants also completed a postquestionnaire, which is not relevant to the present report (described in DePaulo et al., 1996).

The Study 1 participants returned to the lab to complete these forms. Afterward, they were interviewed by one of the investigators, who tried to determine the extent to which the participants had understood and complied with the procedure and believed the information they had been given about the research. This extensive interview uncovered no problems with the procedure. Therefore, in Study 2, all of the forms from this phase of the study were mailed to the participants, and a written debrief (plus payment) was included in the package. Participants returned the materials in an addressed and stamped envelope that was also included in the package.

Self-Centered and Other-Oriented Lies

As described in detail in DePaulo et al. (1996) , the reasons participants gave for telling each of their lies were coded into the two major categories of self-centered and other-oriented. (The kappas were .69 and .68.) A third category of "neither self-centered nor other-oriented" was also coded, but those results are not relevant to the present report. That category included lies told to control an interaction, to create an effect (e.g., to entertain), to conform to conventions, or to simplify a response. Also coded but not included in the analyses were instances in which participants said they did not know why they told the lie. Examples of self-centered and other-oriented lies are shown in Table 1 .

Table 1

Examples of Self-Centered and Other-Oriented Lies Told to People in Different Relationship Categories

Relationship Category	Lie	Reason
	Self-Centered Lies	
Nonromantic		
Best friend	I lied about something I didn't want him to know.	I told the lie so I could keep some privacy about my personal life.
Friend	I told her that I admire her uninhibited way.	So she would not think that I was a prude.
Acquaintance	I said I was not worried about my grades.	I didn't want him to think I was stupid. That I am so smart that it is easy to pull them up.
Stranger	Told customer that if she likes her jeans that way, they weren't too tight.	To sell the outfit. (I did.)
Romantic partner	Said I didn't mind him picking up a girl last night.	Wanted to appear untouchable.
(not spouse)		
Family		
Mother	I told her I'd been studying hard.	Because she's my mother and she'd kill me if she thought I hadn't been studying.
Father	Said we paid off all bills except standard monthly, but we haven't.	So he would co-sign for a new house I want even though he thinks it's too much money.
Spouse	I told her I had to be in D.C. to see a doctor.	Actually, I wanted to visit a friend to trade computer software.
Child	Told son to clean up room and get ready for the weekend and maybe we'd do something special.	Needed his room cleaned up.

(continued on next page)

(Table 1 *continued*)

Other-Oriented lies

Nonromantic

Best friend	I told her that I'd love for her to stay with me and my family if she wanted to when I really wanted to be alone with them.	She was lonely and I didn't want her to have to stay in the dorm by herself.
Friend	Took sides with her when I really think she was also at fault.	She's going through a divorce and I just didn't want to go against her because it's hard enough to deal with a divorce.
Acquaintance	I told her she was nice-looking even though she isn't.	To make her feel good.
Stranger	Acted like I didn't know the information she was giving me. She told me to "talk to so and so." (I already had talked to so and so.)	So she could feel helpful.
Romantic partner *(not spouse)*	Told him I loved the food he ordered for me when it wasn't that great.	Didn't want to make him feel bad.

Family

Mother	I told her I didn't mind going shopping if she wanted me to.	She needs my help but wouldn't ask if she thought I didn't want to go.
Father	I hid my wife's plans to leave.	He would be hurt by the truth and my wife may change her mind.
Spouse	After sex, I pretended to have experienced orgasm.	Did not want to hurt my husband.
Child	I told my son maybe my husband was late because he had car trouble when I thought he'd stopped off for a drink.	Didn't want my son to worry.

Self-centered lies

Self-centered lies were defined as lies told to protect or enhance the liars psychologically or to advantage or protect the liars' interests (as described below). Also included were lies told to elicit a particular emotional response that the liars desired.

The lies told for psychological reasons included lies told to protect the liars from embarrassment, loss of face, or looking bad; from disapproval or having their feelings hurt; and from worry, conflict, or other unpleasantness. They also included lies told to protect the liars' privacy; to make the liars appear better (or just different) than they are; and to regulate the liars' own feelings, emotions, and moods.

The lies told for reasons of personal advantage included lies told for the liars' personal gain, to make things easier or more pleasant for the liars, or to help them get information or get their way. They also included lies told to protect the liars from physical punishment, or to protect their property or assets or their safety. Lies told to protect the liars from loss of status or position or to protect them from being bothered or from doing something they preferred not to do were also included.

Other-oriented lies

Other-oriented lies were defined as lies told to protect or enhance other persons psychologically or to advantage or protect the interests of others (as described below). Lies told to bother or annoy others or to cause them psychological damage (e.g., lie: "Told him the boss wanted to talk to him, but he really didn't"; reason: "so he'd look like a fool") were not included. Only 0.84% of the lies in Study 1 and 2.39% in Study 2 were of this nasty variety.

The other-oriented lies told for psychological reasons included lies told to protect another person from embarrassment, loss of face, or looking bad; from disapproval or having their feelings hurt; from worry, conflict, or other unpleasantness. They also included lies told to protect another person's privacy; to make other people appear better (or just different) than they are; and to regulate another person's feelings, emotions, or moods.

The lies told for another person's advantage included lies told for another person's personal gain, to make things easier or more pleasant for others, to be accommodating, or to help them get their way. They also included lies told to protect others from physical punishment, or to protect their property or assets or their safety. Lies to protect others from loss of status or position or to protect them from being bothered or from doing something they preferred not to do were also included.

Results

Sample Characteristics: Closeness, Duration, and Frequency

Because we were interested in predicting rates of lying from the quality of participants' relationships with particular other people, we included in our analyses only those lies told to just one person (dyadic lies) and omitted those lies that were told to more than one person at a time. Dyadic lies constituted 61% of the lies told by the college students and 72% of the lies told by the community members.

Table 2 shows the mean level of closeness, the mean duration of the relationship, and the mean frequency of interaction with partners in each relationship category. (Fathers are not included as a separate category in the table because only 11 community members and 15 college students reported having any dyadic interactions with their fathers over the course of the week. Fathers are, however, included in the composite category of all family members.) The college students and community members were remarkably similar in their self-reported closeness to different categories of relationship partners, both in the rank ordering of the categories and the absolute values of the means. Both groups reported extremely high levels of closeness to their best friends, family members, and romantic partners. They also reported fairly high levels of closeness to their friends and very low levels of closeness to acquaintances and strangers. The community members, who were older than the college students, reported relationships of longer duration than those of the college students in every category except strangers. The rank ordering of the relationship types by duration, however, was identical for the two groups. With regard to the frequency of their interactions, the college students reported relatively more interactions with friends than did the community members, $t(137) = 4.03$, $p < .001$, whereas the community members reported relatively more interactions with acquaintances, $t(121) = 3.22$, $p = .002$, and family members, $t(112) = 6.69$, $p < .001$.

Table 2

Mean Closeness, Duration, and Frequency of Interacting for Different Categories of Relationships

Relationship category	n^a	Closeness[b]	Duration[c]	Duration[d]	Frequency[e]
Nonromantic					
Best friend					
College	46	13.93	3.79	5.99	5.48
Community	25	13.43	8.51	9.23	4.68
Friend					
College	77	9.90	1.41	3.29	13.29
Community	62	9.41	4.23	6.00	7.94
Acquaintance					
College	64	4.57	0.41	1.77	3.36
Community	59	4.57	2.18	3.99	6.00
Stranger					
College	14	1.42	0.04	0.51	1.36
Community	27	1.34	0.05	0.36	1.30
All friends					
College	77	10.66	1.74	3.65	16.56
Community	64	9.98	4.68	6.34	9.52
All acq/str					
College	67	4.27	0.38	1.67	3.49
Community	60	4.21	1.98	3.57	6.48
Romantic (not spouse)					
College	59	13.48	2.28	4.44	6.36
Community	28	13.31	4.35	6.54	9.18
Family					
(All)					
College	54	14.02	18.21	14.67	2.35
Community	60	13.31	20.15	14.78	8.80
Mother					
College	39	14.53	18.83	15.03	1.64
Community	22	13.58	29.00	18.50	2.27
Spouse					
Community	30	14.42	18.30	13.76	8.07
Child					
Community	23	14.15	15.30	12.49	5.43
All Partners[f]					
College	77	10.31	2.92	4.29	1.99
Community	69	9.23	6.80	7.10	2.20

Correlations among the closeness, duration, and frequency of social interaction variables were computed separately for each participant, weighted by the number of partners, then averaged. (In all analyses to follow, a square root transformation was applied to the number of months of relationship longevity to form our duration measure.) Closeness was significantly correlated with duration (square root), $r (76) = .52$, $p < .001$, for the college students, and $r (68) = .56$, $p < .001$, for the community members, and with frequency, $r (76) = .33$, $p < .001$, for the college students, and $r (68) = .43$, $p < .001$, for the community members. Duration and frequency were not significantly correlated for either sample. r s = .04 and .24, respectively.[3]

Predicting Rate of Lying and Types of Lies From Closeness, Duration, and Frequency

One of the primary questions addressed in this study is whether the rate of lying to a partner relates to the closeness of the relationship between the participant and that partner. The rate of lying data have an unbalanced hierarchical structure such that each participant interacts with (and lies to) different partners, and some participants have interactions with many partners whereas other participants interact with relatively few partners. This hierarchically nested data structure can be analyzed using a multilevel regression approach (Kenny, Kashy, & Bolger, in press). This method of analysis involves two steps, the first of which estimates the relationship between closeness to a partner and rate of lying to that partner separately for each participant. The second step aggregates the relationship between closeness and rate of lying to the partner across participants and tests whether, across participants, the closeness and rate of lying relationship is statistically different from zero. The second step can also be used to examine whether this relationship differs as a function of participant-level predictor variables, such as participant gender.

Consider as an example the relationship between rate of lying (number of lies to the partner divided by number of social interactions with the partner) and relationship duration. Each participant generates two scores for each partner: the rate of lying to that partner and the length of time the participant has known the partner. In the multilevel modeling approach, a separate regression equation is estimated for each participant in which duration predicts rate of lying;

interaction partner is the unit of analysis in each participant's regression. These regressions yield both an intercept and a slope for each participant. Interpretation of the intercepts from the multilevel approach is simplified if the predictor variable(s), relationship duration in this example, is centered around zero or standardized. The intercept estimates the participant's average rate of lying across all partners, and the slope estimates the relationship between how long a participant has known a partner and the rate of lying to that partner.

The regression coefficients (intercepts and slopes) estimated for each participant then serve as outcome measures in a second set of regression analyses that treat participant as the unit of analysis. This step of the analysis can include participant-level predictor variables, such as participant gender. In one second-step regression analysis, the intercepts from the first-step regressions are used as the criterion scores. If participant gender is used as a predictor (coded as men $= -1$, women $= 1$), this second-step regression would yield an estimate of the grand mean for rate of lying, as well as an estimate of the degree to which male participants lied more or less frequently than female participants. More important, when the slopes from the first-step regressions are used as the criterion scores and participant gender is the predictor, the second-step regression yields an intercept that estimates the average relationship between relationship duration and rate of lying for all participants. This analysis also provides an estimate of the degree to which the relationship between relationship duration and rate of lying differs for male and female participants.

The precision of the first-step regressions is likely to vary from participant to participant for two reasons. First, some partic- ipants will have interacted with more partners than others. Second, the relationship between relationship duration and rate of lying may be more consistent for some participants than for others. The two-step regression approach used in our analyses takes these factors into account using a weighted least-squares solution in which the second step regressions are weighted by the standard errors of the first step regression coefficients.

This two-step regression approach was used to examine the relationship between each measure of closeness and rate of lying. We also used a variation on this approach to examine the unique predictive ability of each of the three closeness variables, partialing out the other two. That is, for each participant a multiple regression equation was estimated in which rate of lying to a particular partner was the criterion and subjective closeness to the partner, duration of relationship, and frequency of interaction with the partner were entered simultaneously in the first step regressions. The regression coefficients from these multiple regressions were then pooled across participants, again weighting by the standard errors of the regression coefficients. In the results and discussion below, each of the predictor variables was standardized.

Results for both the univariate and multivariate methods are shown in Table 3 .4 We also combined the results of the college and community samples using the meta-analytic technique of combining p s. When the results were not significant for one or both samples but were significant in the combined analysis, we mention the combined p in the text.

Table 3

Predicting Rate of Lying and Types of Lies From Closeness, Duration, and Frequency of Interaction

Variable	Regression with 1 relationship variable[a]		Simultaneous regression with all 3 variables[b]	
	b	*t*	*b*	*t*
	Rate of lying[c]			
Closeness				
College	-.084	4.99***	-.106	5.15***
Community	-.063	3.00**	-.055	2.07*
Duration[d]				
College	-.010	0.60	.033	1.78+
Community	-.039	2.07*	.016	0.65
Frequency of interaction				
College	-.036	2.42*	-.014	0.91
Community	-.045	4.47**	.001	0.05
	Self-centered lies[e]			
Closeness				
College	-.064	2.56**	-.104	2.92**
Community	.050	1.01	.076	0.71
Duration[d]				
College	-.028	0.91	-.021	0.57
Community	.023	0.41	.080	0.80
Frequency of interaction				
College	-.002	0.09	.043	1.40
Community	.030	0.73	.094	1.49
	Other-oriented lies[f]			
Closeness				
College	.073	2.74**	.069	2.05*
Community	.050	1.38	.071	1.01
Duration[d]				
College	.071	2.87**	.065	1.83+
Community	-.007	0.14	-.113	1.45
Frequency of interaction				
College	.010	0.40	-.038	1.09
Community	-.001	0.04	-.057	0.90

Note to Table 3. Analyses of rate of lying were based on college: n = 71 and community: n = 59. Analyses of self-centered lies were based on college: n = 41 and community: n = 21. Analyses of other-oriented lies were based on college: n = 34 and community: n = 21.

[a] Two-step regression analyses with closeness or duration or frequency entered in the first step and participant gender in the second.

[b] Simultaneous regression with closeness, duration, and frequency entered together in the first step and participant gender in the second.

[c] Number of lies told to partner divided by number of social interactions with partner.

[d] Analyses were based on square root of number of months.

[e] Number of self-centered lies told to partner divided by the total number of lies told to partner.

[f] Number of other-oriented lies told to partner divided by the total number of lies told to partner.

$+ p <$ or $= .10$. $* p <$ or $= .05$. $** p <$ or $= .01$. $*** p <$ or $= .001$.

In the analyses that included just one of the relationship variables at a time, closeness, relationship duration, and frequency of social interaction were all (negative) predictors of the overall rate of lying and were significantly so for all except duration for the college students. Participants told fewer lies to the people in their lives to whom they felt closer, to those with whom they interacted more frequently, and (for the community members) to those whom they had known for a longer time. However, when all three variables were entered simultaneously, only closeness remained a significant predictor of lying. For both groups, partic- ipants lied less often to the people to whom they felt closer. The relationship variables did not interact significantly with either participant gender or partner gender.

The proportion of lies that were self-centered was not significantly predicted by either duration or frequency. For the college student sample, it was predicted by closeness: When participants told lies to the people in their lives to whom they felt especially close, relatively fewer of those lies were self-centered ones. However, a significant interaction of closeness with participant gender, t (40) = 2.24, p = .031, indicated that it was primarily for the men that closeness was a negative predictor of the proportion of self-centered lies (for men, the coefficient for closeness predicting rate of lying was −.12); for women, there was essentially no relationship (b = −.008). No other interactions with gender were significant.

As predicted, closeness was a positive predictor of the rate of telling other-oriented lies. When participants did tell lies to the people to whom they felt especially close, relatively more of those lies were other-oriented ones. This effect was in the same direction for both samples and was significant for the college students and in the combined analysis (the combined p = .006). The only other significant predictor of the telling of other-oriented lies was duration: For the college students (only), the longer they had known another person, the more likely it was that the lies they told to that person would be other-oriented ones.[5]

64

For some family members, the duration of the relationship is sometimes equal to the participant's age. Therefore, for all results involving relationship duration, we recomputed them deleting family members. For rate of lying in the single-variable regression, the result for duration that was significant for the community sample became nonsignificant when family members were excluded, $b = -.028$, $t(54) = 1.24$, $p = .22$. For the simultaneous regression, the result for duration for the college sample that was marginally significant became nonsignificant, $b = .025$, $t(68) = 1.27$, $p = .21$. For predictions of self-centered lies for the community sample, the result for the single-variable regression for duration that was in the unpredicted direction (positive) became negative, though not significantly so, $b = -.041$, $t(18) = 0.97$, $p = .34$. In the simultaneous regression, the b for duration for the community sample also became slightly negative, $b = -.015$, $t(10) = 0.18$, $p = .86$. For predictions of other-oriented lies for the college sample, the result for duration in the single-variable regression dropped from significant to nearly significant, $b = .048$, $t(29) = 1.76$, $p = .09$. For the community sample, the result for duration in the single-variable regression that was in the unpredicted direction (negative) became positive and significant, $b = .075$, $t(20) = 2.14$, $p = .04$. For the simultaneous regression for the community sample, the result for duration also switched from negative to slightly positive, $b = .032$, $t(11) = 0.58$, $p = .57$. In sum, when analyses involving relationship duration were recomputed deleting family members, the results for rate of lying became slightly weaker, but the results for self-centered and other-oriented lying generally became somewhat more consistent with predictions.

Lying in Different Kinds of Relationships

Table 4 shows the overall rate of lying and the proportions of lies that were self-centered and other-oriented separately for each of the different kinds of relationship. In these analyses, we separated romantic relationships and family relationships from other relationships. We predicted that within the latter category, the overall rate of lying would be lowest for best friends, next lowest for friends, then acquaintances, and would be highest for strangers. In that closeness systematically decreased from best friends to strangers (see Table 2), this was another test of the closeness hypothesis, only with romantic and family ties removed. The ordering of the means for both groups was generally as predicted by the closeness hypothesis. The overall rate of lying increased systematically from best friends and friends to acquaintances and strangers. The linear trend was tested using a multilevel regression approach in which a regression equation was computed for each participant using the level of the relationship as a predictor (best friend = 4, friend = 3, acquaintance = 2, and stranger = 1) and the rate of lying to partners in that relationship category as the criterion. The test of the linear slope was significant for both groups, $t(41) = 2.83$, $p = .007$, for the college students and $t(24) = 2.15$, $p = .042$, for the community members.

65

Table 4

Rate of Lying and Types of Lies in Different Categories of Relationships

Relationship category	Rate of lying[a] Mean	n	Self-centered lies[b] Mean	n	Other-oriented lies[c] Mean	n
Nonromantic						
Best friend						
College	27.96	46	37.28	23	36.67	23
Community	17.03	25	50.00	7	42.86	7
Friend						
College	27.62	77	38.16	61	28.29	61
Community	26.06	62	42.84	37	42.78	37
Acquaintance						
College	48.21	64	56.40	43	13.72	43
Community	32.86	59	55.78	36	24.27	36
Stranger						
College	77.38	14	54.54	11	18.18	11
Community	55.56	27	54.49	13	26.28	13
All friends						
College	27.47	77	38.31	63	30.22	63
Community	21.71	64	42.18	38	44.46	38
All acq/str						
College	48.31	67	58.26	44	14.39	44
Community	35.34	60	54.85	39	23.72	39
Romantic (not spouse)						
College	34.33	59	47.27	37	28.22	37
Community	31.78	28	64.22	17	19.61	17
Family						
(All)						
College	31.53	54	48.96	24	34.38	24
Community	15.36	60	60.77	29	18.94	29
Mother						
College	46.37	39	58.33	20	31.67	20
Community	30.08	22	66.67	9	11.11	9
Spouse						
Community	9.85	30	46.50	10	16.50	10
Child						
Community	8.08	23	65.48	7	34.52	7

[a] Number of lies divided by number of social interactions multiplied by 100.
[b] Number of self-centered lies divided by total number of lies multiplied by 100.
[c] Number of other-oriented lies divided by total number of lies multiplied by 100.

We combined best friends and friends into a category called "all friends," and compared the rate of lying to that category with the rate of lying to the category of acquaintances and strangers combined. This test was significant for both groups (see Table 5). The college students and the community members told more lies per social interaction to acquaintances and strangers than to their friends. Comparisons of the category of all family members to the acquaintance plus stranger composite yielded a significant result for the community members, who reported a lower rate of lying to their family members than to acquaintances and strangers. The effect was in the same direction for the college students, and it was significant in the combined analysis ($p = .003$). Finally, the rate of lying to family members did not differ significantly from the rate of lying to all friends for either sample.

Table 5

Comparison of Lies Told to Family, Friends, and Acquaintances and Strangers

	Rate of lying[a]		Self-centered lies[b]		Other-oriented lies[c]	
Comparison	*t*	n	*t*	n	*t*	n
Friends versus acq/str						
College	2.75**	67	1.78+	39	3.00**	39
Community	2.20*	55	2.12*	25	3.29**	25
Acq/str versus family						
College	1.39	48	1.31	17	1.69	17
Community	2.99**	51	0.27	16	0.03	16
Friends versus family						
College	0.42	54	1.49	22	0.46	22
Community	1.24	55	1.11	18	2.09*	18

Note to Table 5. Acq/str = acquaintances and strangers.
[a] Number of lies divided by number of social interactions multiplied by 100.
[b] Number of self-centered lies divided by total number of lies multiplied by 100.
[c] Number of other-oriented lies divided by total number of lies multiplied by 100.
$+ p <$ or $= .10.$ $* p <$ or $+ .05.$ $** p <$ or $= .01.$

Although participants in both groups reported high levels of closeness to their romantic partners and to their mothers, the rates of lying in both of these categories were fairly high. Both the college students and community members told about one lie in every three of their social interactions to their romantic partners (not including spouses). The rate of lying to mother was especially high for the college students and approached the level of one lie in every two social interactions. In contrast, the rates of lying to spouses and children were the lowest of all: The community members told less than one lie in every 10 social interactions to them.

We could not compute the linear contrast on the proportions of all lies that were self-centered or other-oriented, because the number of participants who told those kinds of lies to partners in several different relationship categories was too small. However, we did compute the critical comparison between all friends and the acquaintance and stranger composite. This comparison was significant or nearly so for both samples and for both kinds of lies. As predicted, participants told proportionately fewer self-centered lies and proportionally more other-oriented lies to their friends than to acquaintances and strangers.

To determine whether the key relationship between closeness and overall rate of lying (shown in Table 3) would also occur within each of the relationship categories, we computed regressions using closeness as a predictor of number of lies per social interaction for the categories of (a) best friends and friends, (b) acquaintances and strangers, and (c) all family members. The n s for these analyses are necessarily smaller than those in Table 3 because only a subset of the relationship categories is included each time. In addition, the n s are reduced because some participants did not have multiple interactions within a relationship category (or did not lie to anyone in that relationship category) and were therefore not included in the analyses of that category. Also, participants who assigned identical closeness ratings to all of their partners within a given category had to be excluded as well. Consequently, we did not have sufficient n s to compute these regressions for the all family category for the college students (we had an n of 14 for the community sample). The other n s, for the college and community samples respectively, were 70 and 38 for best friends and friends, and 22 and 25 for acquaintances and strangers.

For four of the five slopes that we could compute, the predicted negative relationship between closeness and rate of lying occurred. Only for the all family category in the community sample was the slope positive, b = .011, but the effect was tiny, t (13) = 0.10, p = .92. For the category of all friends, the b s were −.015 and −.040 for the college and community samples. Although neither of these effects reached significance (p s = .26 and .12), the combined p was nearly significant (p = .058). Similarly, within the category of acquaintances and strangers, the b s were −.067 and −.064, which were individually nonsignificant (p s = .20 and .21) but nearly significant when combined (p = .071). In sum, within all of the major relationship categories, except the family category for the community sample, the key finding that fewer lies were told to closer relationship partners was replicated. That the significance levels were not as impressive as in the analyses using all of the data is attributable to the reduced power.

68

Perhaps what is important about lying in relationships is not the rate of lying, but whether any lies at all are told to a particular relationship partner. To examine this possibility, we looked at the percentage of partners within each category to whom any lies at all were told. For the college students, these percentages were 66, 44, 36, and 38, respectively, for the strangers, acquaintances, friends, and best friends. For the community members, the corresponding values were 47, 34, 30, and 33. (The percentage for the category of all family members was identical for both samples, 34.) In both samples, participants told lies to a smaller percentage of their best friends and friends than to acquaintances and strangers; for the college students, $t (67) = 1.72$, $p = .090$, for the community members, $t (57) = 2.12$, $p = .038$ (combined $p = .008$). The linear trend testing the prediction that participants would tell the greatest percentage of lies to strangers, next greatest to acquaintances, and lowest to best friends was nearly significant in each sample, $b = -.051$, $t (47) = 1.80$, $p = .078$, for the college students, and $b = -.078$, $t (27) = 1.96$, $p = .06$, for the community members, and was significant in the combined analysis ($p = .010$). In sum, considering the percentage of partners to whom any lies were told instead of the number of lies per social interaction does not change the conclusion that lying decreases as relationship closeness increases.

Predicting Characteristics of the Lies From Closeness, Duration, and Frequency

Multilevel regression analyses were used to predict characteristics of the lies (e.g., degree of planning, importance of avoiding detection) using relationship closeness, relationship duration, and frequency of interaction as predictors. As described earlier, in this analysis a separate regression was computed for each participant, treating partner as the unit of analysis. In this case, however, the criterion was the average rating of a lie characteristic to a particular partner, averaging across all lies told to that partner. The predictor was the variable measuring closeness of the relationship (standardized) with the partner. As before, the second step of the analysis involved predicting the regression coefficients from the first step, using participant gender as the predictor. This analysis resulted in an average regression coefficient estimating the relationship between the lie characteristic variable and the closeness measure (see Table 6), as well as an estimate of the interaction between participant gender and partner closeness in predicting the lie characteristic.

Table 6

Predicting Characteristics of the Lies From Closeness, Duration, and Frequency of Interaction

Lie characteristic	Closeness b	Duration b^a	Frequency b
Distress before			
College	.179*	.171	.328
Community	.110	.376+	-.725+
Distress during			
College	.060	.202+	.419*
Community	.023	.427	-.697+
Distress after			
College	.131	.233*	.377+
Community	.115	.265	-.509+
Target believed			
College	-.282**	-.182	.012
Community	.040	.116	.124
Was it discovered?			
College	.092**	.017	-.049
Community	.092	.189	-.345*

Note to Table 6. The regression coefficients (*b*s) above were computed using standardized predictor variables.
[a] Analyses were based on square root of number of months.
+ $p <$ or $= .10$.   * $p <$ or $= .05$.   ** $p <$ or $= .01$.

Table 6 shows the regression coefficients for the predictions of the characteristics of the lies for the two samples. We predicted that participants would feel more distressed about the lies that they told to their closer relationship partners. For the key variable of subjective closeness, all six results (distress before, during, and after, for the college and community samples) were in the predicted direction. For distress before, the b s were significant for the college students and in the combined analysis (p = .04), and for distress after, the combined result was nearly significant (p = .06). Generally, then, the participants did feel more uncomfortable about the lies they told to the people to whom they felt emotionally closer, though most of the individual results (before combining) were not significant.

The duration of the relationship was a consistent predictor of participants' distress across both samples. The college students and the community members felt more distressed before (combined p = .02), during (combined p = .02), and after (combined p = .01) the telling of their lies to the people they had known longer. However, when these analyses were recomputed omitting family members, all of the results became nonsignificant.

70

The results for frequency were in different directions for the two samples. The college students tended to feel more distressed about the lies that they told to the people with whom they interacted more frequently. The community members tended to feel less distressed about their lies to those people.

We also predicted that participants would feel less confident that their lies had been believed when the targets of those lies were closer relationship partners. For the college students, the result for subjective closeness was as predicted. No other effects were significant.

Finally, we predicted that the lies would be more likely to have been discovered by the end of the study when they had been told to partners to whom the participants felt emotionally closer, whom the participants had known longer, and with whom they interacted more frequently. For subjective closeness, the results were in the predicted direction for both groups and were significant for the college students and in the combined analysis ($p = .01$). For relationship duration, the results were in the predicted direction but not significant. (This was also true when family members were excluded from the analyses.) For frequency, the results were in the direction contrary to predictions and were significant for the community members and in the combined analysis ($p = .05$). There were no significant interactions with participant gender for any of the lie characteristics.

In sum, the results for the characteristics of the lies were strongest and most consistent with predictions for the measure of subjective closeness. Participants tended to feel more distressed before and after telling lies to people to whom they felt emotionally closer. At the time that they told their lies, the college students were especially unlikely to think that their subjectively closer relationship partners believed those lies. And across both groups, participants reported that the lies they told to their subjectively closer relationship partners were more likely to have been discovered by the end of the study.

Characteristics of Lies in Different Kinds of Relationships

We computed the mean level of each lie characteristic separately for each of the three relationship category composites: all friends, acquaintances plus strangers, and all family members. We then did pairwise comparisons and combined the p values across the two samples. For the comparisons of friends with acquaintances and strangers, there were no effects that were significant and consistent across the two groups. For the college students, one effect was consistent with predictions: They thought that their friends were less likely to have believed their lies than were acquaintances and strangers, $t(37) = -2.36$, $p = .02$. For the comparisons of lies told to family members versus acquaintances and strangers, participants' feelings of distress during and after the telling of their lies were in the same direction for both samples and were significant in the combined analysis. As predicted, participants felt more distressed during and after the telling of their lies to family members, relative to acquaintances and strangers. For distress during, for the college students, $t(15) = 2.38$, $p = .03$; for the community members, $t(15) = 1.62$, $p = .13$; and the combined $p = .01$. For distress after, for the college students, $t(16) = 1.29$, $p = .22$; for the community members, t (15) = 1.92, p = .07; and the combined p = .03. Finally, for comparisons of lies told to family members with lies told to friends, only one effect was significant: The college students said that they felt more distressed while lying to family members than to their friends, t (21) = −2.72, p = .01.

Discussion

Closeness Predicts Lower Rates of Everyday Lying

Among the qualities that people value most in their close personal relationships are the self-disclosure and confiding that occur in those relationships, the freedom they feel to be themselves (Argyle & Henderson, 1984 ; Maxwell, 1985 ; Parks & Floyd, 1996), and their trust that their partners will care about them and be responsive to their needs. The same characteristics predict the quality and durability of personal relationships (Argyle & Henderson, 1984 ; Hendrick, 1981). Those characteristics are also described as deeply significant in some of the most influential theoretical statements about close relationships (e.g., Bowlby, 1988 ; Deci & Ryan, 1991 ; Hazan & Shaver, 1994 ; Holmes & Rempel, 1989).

In contrast, the lies that people tell in their everyday social interactions violate just those ideals. When people tell everyday lies, they pretend to be different kinds of people than they believe they really are, and they profess feelings that they are not actually experiencing and opinions they do not in fact embrace (DePaulo et al., 1996). We therefore expected to find lower rates of lying to closer relationship partners. The data were strongly supportive of that prediction. In both studies, when we examined the relationship between closeness and rates of lying for all of the people with whom the participants interacted, we found that the participants told fewer lies per social interaction to the people to whom they felt closer. Participants also told fewer lies to the people with whom they interacted more frequently, and for the community members, they told fewer lies to the people they had known longer. But when all of these relational aspects—closeness, frequency of interacting, and relational duration—were considered simultaneously, it was subjective closeness that emerged as the only significant predictor of rates of lying. It was also subjective closeness that most consistently predicted participants' feeling of discomfort about their lies. Participants felt more distressed before and after telling lies to partners to whom they felt emotionally closer.

Our position, then, is that everyday lies violate the nature of close relationships. If people's presentations of themselves to another person are so distorted as to be deliberately misleading, and if they hide and fake their feelings and opinions a bit too often, then their relationship with that person may no longer be a close one. Ideally, close relationships should provide some insulation from the need to present oneself dishonestly. People in close relationships know each other's weaknesses and annoyances as well as their strengths and charms, and yet they still value and care about each other. Reis and Patrick's (1996) account of the intimacy process highlights the importance of feeling understood and validated. Perhaps those feelings are what separate relationships that are emotionally close from those that are characterized only by longevity or by

72

frequent contacts. Duration of the relationship and frequency of interaction by themselves provide little protection from the risks of honestly presenting one's true and vulnerable self.

Pragmatic Deterrents to Lying

Although we believe that the emotional deterrents to lie telling in close relationships are most important, we think that there are important practical considerations as well. Partners in emotionally close relationships believe that they develop special sensitivities to each other's verbal and nonverbal cues and that they are therefore especially likely to see through each other's lies (Anderson et al., in press). Even in instances when close relationship partners believe that they might get away with their lies when they first tell them, they may still fear that the lies will be detected eventually or that the work of maintaining the lies would not be worth the effort. There are also certain lies that simply cannot be told to close relationship partners, who are already knowledgeable about the truth of the matter. All of these kinds of factors could have helped to account for our finding that people told fewer lies per social interaction to their closer relationship partners.

If participants were in fact deterred from telling lies that they believed had little chance of remaining undetected by their close relationship partners, then perhaps the lies they did tell were more successful. But that did not occur. The college students thought that their emotionally closer relationship partners were less likely to have believed their lies at the time they were told. They and the community members, considered together, also reported that the lies they told to their closer relationship partners were more likely eventually to have been discovered. We had predicted that lies would also be more often discovered by partners the participants had known for a long time, and by partners with whom the participants interacted frequently. We were wrong on both counts. We thought that frequent interactions would provide frequent opportunities to discover the lies and that longevity would provide relationship partners with an accumulated knowledge about each other that would also increase the odds that lies would eventually come undone. But neither opportunity nor knowledge may matter much if emotional investment is lacking. Perhaps relationship partners need to care about knowing the true facts and feelings of each other's lives in order to turn opportunity and knowledge into insight and lie-detection success.

The Special Place of Altruistic Lies in Close Relationships

In underscoring the link between honesty and closeness, we are not denying the presence and importance of deception in personal relationships (see also DePaulo, 1992 ; Parks, 1982). Even in relationships with spouses, for which the rate of lying was lower than for any other adult category, lies were told in nearly one out of every 10 social interactions. Efforts to eliminate totally all everyday lies from close personal relationships would probably be misguided. For instance, a little bit of light lying might serve important privacy needs for individuals in close relationships.

Other important functions of lying were suggested by the special place that altruistic lies seem to hold in close relationships. Although lying in general, and—in some analyses—self-centered lying in particular, occurs at lower rates in closer relationships, other-oriented lying occurs at relatively higher rates. People who tell the kinds of other-oriented lies that involve faking agreement with their partner's opinion or course of action may be conveying the message that they are on their partner's side. In discussing the importance of talk to the maintenance of relationships, Duck (1994) argues that talk serves to demonstrate a "symbolic union" between the relationship partners. Our data suggest that when partners in close relationships are not in fact united in their views, they may still pretend that they are.

Other kinds of altruistic lies serve to protect other people's faces and feelings. These are the kinds of other-oriented lies that may help to convey the caring and concern that have been deemed so essential to the processes of intimacy (Reis & Patrick, 1996), relatedness (Deci & Ryan, 1991), and attachment (Bowlby, 1988).

We had a hint from our earlier work with this data set that other-oriented lies might play a special role in successful relationships (see also Metts, 1989). In our analyses of individual differences in everyday lying (Kashy & DePaulo, 1996), we found that individuals who reported greater satisfaction with their same-gender relationships characteristically (across all of the people with whom they interacted) told relatively more other-oriented lies than self-centered ones. Of course, that finding was about the ways in which particular individuals differ from each other as liars. We could not have known from that finding alone whether it would follow that people tell relatively more altruistic lies than self-centered ones to their closer relationship partners. Conceptually, though, the findings complement each other.

Perhaps we should have recognized another precursor to our findings in a process that has been shown to predict effective relationship functioning. That process is accommodation (Rusbult, Yovetich, & Verette, 1996). It occurs when people who are the target of a relationship partner's inconsiderate, humiliating, or otherwise destructive behavior do not articulate or act on the intense negative emotion that they experience. Instead, they behave constructively, and express sentiments that are kinder than the ones they really feel. Rusbult and her colleagues believe that this process involves a "transformation of motivation." We believe that it also involves deception.

When, in the process of accommodation, individuals set aside their own self-interest and instead behave more constructively, the target of their altruism is not so much their relationship partner as the relationship itself (Rusbult et al., 1996). But perhaps the liars are beneficiaries as well. Aron and his colleagues have argued that in close relationships, individuals behave as if some or all of the characteristics of their partner are also, at least in part, their own. That is, they feel more of a oneness or union with their partner (Aron, Aron, Tudor, & Nelson, 1991). One implication is that acts that benefit the partner are also experienced as beneficial to the individuals themselves. This casts a new light on our findings. It suggests that people may tell relatively more other-oriented lies to their closer relationship partners because they are more likely to feel personally benefited by those lies.

Our argument has been that people tell relatively more altruistic lies in their closer personal relationships because they care more about their partners' feelings in those relationships. These lies, we believe, communicate understanding, validation, and caring—the essential components of intimacy. But in their discussion of the process of developing and maintaining intimacy, Reis and Patrick (1996) noted that partners can validate each other's experiences without necessarily agreeing with their point of view. The implication, it seems, is that it should be possible to communicate caring and concern without lying. This lofty ideal may be admirable, but it is not always easy to achieve. If you really think your friend was at fault in her disastrous relationship with her husband, and that your best friend, who is dying of cancer, looks even worse than she did a few weeks before, how do you communicate those sentiments in a caring, validating, loving—and honest—way?

The Problem With Mothers and Lovers

There were some important exceptions to our findings that closeness predicted lower rates of lying. Participants reported very high levels of closeness to their mothers and to their romantic partners (who were not spouses). Levels of closeness to mothers and lovers were about as high as for best friends, and even higher than for friends. Yet the rates of lying to these partners were not especially low. Participants in both studies told about one lie in every three social interactions to their romantic partners, and community members lied at about the same rate to their mothers. The college students lied in almost every other interaction they had with their mothers. We think that these exceptions occurred because closeness is not the only important predictor of lying. Lying may also be predicted by the power of the targets of the lies (Hample, 1980 ; Lippard, 1988), and by their interpersonal attractiveness and appeal. For college students especially, mothers still control significant resources and privileges, and so students lie in order to obtain those things. Children of all ages may also continue to care about what their mothers think of them, and so self-presentational lies continue to be prevalent even among the adults from the community sample.

Romantic partners who are not spouses present a different set of lures for lies. People may want very much to impress their romantic partners and to be loved and admired by them, but they may be insecure about whether they will succeed. This, too, is a recipe for deceit. Uncertain about whether their "true selves" are lovable enough to attract and keep such appealing mates, people present themselves as they wish they were instead of how they believe they are in fact. Our explanations of the mother and lover problems are speculative, though, and in need of further testing.

Lying and Relationship Development

In comparing the rates of lying to different categories of relationship partners, we were especially struck by the differences between romantic partners who were or were not spouses. People lied in about one out of every three of their interactions with their romantic partners who were not spouses, but in less than one in ten of their interactions with their spouses. As intimate relationships deepen and romantic partners become spouses, do the rates of lying decrease along the way? Or are those romantic relationships that ultimately result in marriage characterized by greater honesty from the outset? Longitudinal studies would help to elucidate these and other possible explanations.

Is the Truth Bias Really a Bias?

One of the most robust findings in the literature on deception–detection is a truth bias: When presented with equal numbers of truths and lies to judge, people characteristically believe that more of the messages are truths than lies (DePaulo, Stone, & Lassiter, 1985). This truth bias is even stronger for close relationship partners, such as relatives and friends, than it is for strangers (Buller, Strzyzewski, & Comstock, 1991 ; Millar & Millar, 1995 ; see also Levine & McCornack, 1992 ; McCornack & Parks, 1986 ; for a review, see Anderson, Ansfield, & DePaulo, in press). Within the experimental paradigms in which the truth bias has been documented, it is indeed an error: People identify more of the messages as truths than lies when in fact the numbers are identical. But in the real world, truths are more common than lies (DePaulo et al., 1996). The present research has shown that rates of truth telling are not equivalent across relationships but are higher in closer relationships. Using real-world base rates as criteria, the stronger truth bias in closer relationship categories should not be regarded as a mistake (Funder, 1987).

Little Lies, Big Lies

Millar and Tesser's (1988) model of violated expectations holds that people tell lies when their behavior violates other people's expectations for them. Because close relationship partners have more expectations for each other, the likelihood that expectations will be violated and lies will be told is greater in close relationships than in casual ones. Our findings that fewer lies are told in close relationships are inconsistent with the Millar and Tesser (1988) predictions. Perhaps we were wrong in thinking that a greater number of expectations implies a greater likelihood of expectancy violation; if the expectations are accurate, then they may be violated only rarely. Another possibility is that the violated expectations model may be a more powerful predictor of serious lies than of the everyday lies that were the focus of the present research. Serious lies are often told to cover seriously bad behaviors, such as infidelities (DePaulo, Ansfield, Kirkendol, & Boden, 1997). In those instances, the truth (e.g., that an infidelity occurred) may seem to the liar to pose a greater threat to the relationship than a lie, which the liar might hope will never be discovered (cf. McCornack & Levine, 1990). In everyday lies, in contrast, it is the lie that is more threatening. One person's poor grades, for example, pose less of a threat to a friendship than the person's denial that the grades are poor or that she or he is concerned about them. In short, we believe that the relationship between closeness and lying will depend on whether the truth or a lie would pose a greater threat to the relationship. In the domain of serious lies, it is often the truth that would hurt the most and force a renegotiation of the relationship; in that domain, then, close relationships may be breeding grounds for deceit.

76

Methodological Issues

In this research, we asked people to tell us about an aspect of their own behavior that is considered socially undesirable in their culture. It is important, then, to address the question of whether we can believe these self-reports of lies. The validity issue is one that concerned us deeply from the outset. We did everything we could think of to try to elicit accurate and thorough reports. For example, we had an extensive initial meeting with the participants in which we explained what counted as a lie in great detail and in which we emphasized the importance of accuracy and conscientiousness. We collected participants' diary entries several times throughout the week so that they would record their own behavior soon after it occurred, and we assured them that their anonymity would be protected (see DePaulo et al., 1996, for further details). So far as we know, no prior study of lying in everyday life instituted such procedures for encouraging accuracy.

Several aspects of our findings reassure us of the validity of participants' reports. First, participants reported a high rate of self-centered lying. They did not try to convince us that all or even most of their lies were altruistic. Second, in this report as well as our previous ones (DePaulo et al., 1996 ; Kashy & DePaulo, 1996), the most important findings were impressively similar across the two samples. If participants were misrepresenting their lying, they were doing so in strikingly similar ways in the two very different groups.

Still, it is possible that some motivations were shared by the two groups and thus produced similar, but invalid, results. For example, it is possible that when participants reported more altruistic motivations for the lies that they told to their closer relationship partners, they were simply rationalizing. We think that the best response to these kinds of challenges is to test them experimentally. For example, Bell and DePaulo (1996) experimentally manipulated participants' liking for an art student, who then questioned the participants about their opinions of her work. Consistent with our findings that people tell relatively more altruistic lies to the people to whom they feel closer, the participants who were induced to like the artist more also told more altruistic lies to her (see also DePaulo & Bell, 1996).

Another threat to the validity of our results is that the diary methodology may be a reactive one. For example, perhaps partic- ipants who noticed that they had told many self-centered lies to some of their interaction partners felt less close to those partners as a consequence, and rated their closeness to them accordingly at the end of the study. We do not find this particular challenge troublesome, as it does not explain why we also found fewer self-centered lies to close others when closeness was operationalized by relationship category (i.e., participants told fewer self-centered lies to best friends and friends than to acquaintances and strangers). Of course, it may be possible to generate still other alternative explanations of our findings that follow from the possible reactivity of the diary methodology. Our response again is to encourage experimental tests of any hypotheses that can be tested experimentally.

At the same time, however, it is important to recognize that the most basic questions that motivated this research—e.g., do people tell fewer lies per social interaction to the people in their lives with whom they share closer emotional bonds (as research and theory on close relationships would predict)?—are not testable experimentally. People cannot be randomly assigned to be spouses, parents, or best friends. We think that the diary methodology, despite its limitations, is the best available methodology for testing theoretically motivated questions about the rates and patterns of everyday lying in close and casual relationships.

References

Anderson, D. E., Ansfield, M. E., & DePaulo, B. M. Love's best habit: Deception in the context of relationships. in pressIn P. Philippot, R. S. Feldman, & E. J. Coats (Eds.), *The social context of nonverbal behavior*. Cambridge, England: Cambridge University Press.

Argyle, M. & Henderson, M. (1984). The rules of friendship. *Journal of Social & Personal Relationships, 1,* 211-237.

Aron, A., Aron, E. N. & Smollan, D. (1992). Inclusion of Other in the Self Scale and the structure of interpersonal closeness. *Journal of Personality & Social Psychology, 63,* 596-612 10.1037//0022-3514 .63.4.596.

Aron, A., Aron, E. N., Tudor, M. & Nelson, G. (1991). Close relationships as including other in the self. *Journal of Personality & Social Psychology, 60,* 241-253 10.1037//0022-3514 .60.2.241.

Baumeister, R. F. & Leary, M. R. (1995). The need to belong: Desire for interpersonal attachment as a fundamental human motivation. *Psychological Bulletin, 117,* 497-529.

Baxter, L. & Wilmot, W. (1985). Taboo topics in close relationships. *Journal of Social & Personal Relationships, 2,* 253-269.

Bell, K. L. & DePaulo, B. M. (1996). Liking and lying. *Basic & Applied Social Psychology, 18,* 243-266.

Berscheid, E., Snyder, M., & Omoto, A. M. (1989a). Issues in studying close relationships: Conceptualizing and measuring closeness. In C. Hendrick (Ed.), Review of personality and social psychology: Vol. 10. Close relationships (pp. 63-91). Newbury Park, Ca: Sage.

Berscheid, E., Snyder, M. & Omoto, A. M. (1989b). The Relationship Closeness Inventory: Assessing the closeness of interpersonal relationships. *Journal of Personality & Social Psychology, 57,* 792-807.

Bowlby, J. (1988). A secure base: Parent-child attachment and healthy human development. New York: Basic Books.

Buller, D. B., Strzyzewski, K. D. & Comstock, J. (1991). Interpersonal deception: I.Deceivers' reactions to receivers' suspicions and probing. *Communication Monographs, 58,* 1-24.

Camden, C., Motley, M. T. & Wilson, A. (1984). White lies in interpersonal communication: A taxonomy and preliminary investigation of social motivations. *Western Journal of Speech Communication, 48,* 309-325.

Deci, E. L., & Ryan, R. M. (1991). A motivational approach to self: Integration in personality. In R. Dienstbier (Ed.), *Nebraska Symposium on Motivation: Vol. 38. Perspectives on motivation* (pp. 237-288). Lincoln: University of Nebraska Press.

DePaulo, B. M. (1992). Nonverbal behavior and self-presentation. *Psychological Bulletin, 111,* 203-243.

DePaulo, B. M. & Bell, K. L. (1996). *Journal of Personality & Social Psychology, 71,* 703-716 10.1037//0022-3514 .71.4.703.

DePaulo, B. M., Ansfield, M. E., Kirkendol, S. E., & Boden, J. M. (1997). Serious lies: First person accounts. Manuscript in preparation.

DePaulo, B. M., Kashy, D. A., Kirkendol, S. E., Wyer, M. M. & Epstein, J. A. (1996). Lying in everyday life. *Journal of Personality & Social Psychology, 70,* 979-995.

DePaulo, B. M., Stone, J. I., & Lassiter, G. D. (1985). Deceiving and detecting deceit. In B. R. Schlenker (Ed.), *The self and social life* (pp. 323-370). New York: McGraw-Hill.

Duck, S. (1994). Steady as (s)he goes. In D. Canary & L. Stafford (Eds.), *Communication and relational maintenance* (pp. 45-60). New York: Academic Press.

Ekman, P. & Friesen, W. V. (1969). Nonverbal leakage and clues to deception. *Psychiatry: Interpersonal & Biological Processes, 32,* 88-106.

Funder, D. C. (1987). Errors and mistakes: Evaluating the accuracy of social judgment. *Psychological Bulletin, 101,* 75-90.

Hample, D. (1980). Purposes and effects of lying. *Southern Speech Communication Journal, 46,* 33-47.

Hazan, C. & Shaver, P. R. (1994). Attachment as an organizational framework for research on close relationships. *Psychological Inquiry, 5,* 1-22.

Hendrick, S. S. (1981). Attachment as an organizational framework for research on close relationships. *Journal of Personality & Social Psychology, 40,* 1150-1159.

Holmes, J. G., & Rempel, J. K. (1989). Trust in close relationships. In C. Hendrick (Ed.), Review of personality and social psychology: Vol. 10. *Close relationships* (pp. 187-220). Newbury Park, Ca: Sage.

Kashy, D. A. & DePaulo, B. M. (1996). Who lies? *Journal of Personality & Social Psychology, 70,* 1037-1051.

Kelley, H. H., Berscheid, E., Christensen, A., Harvey, J. H., Huston, T. L., Levinger, G., McClintock, E., Peplau, L. A., & Peterson, D. R. (1983). Analyzing close relationships. In H. H. Kelley, E. Berscheid, A.

Christensen, J. H. Harvey, T. L. Huston, G. Levinger, E. McClintock, L. A. Peplau, & D. R. Peterson (Eds.), *Close relationships* (pp. 20-67). New York: Freeman.

Kenny, D. A., Kashy, D. A., & Bolger, N. Data analysis in social psychology. in press. In D. T. Gilbert, S. T. Fiske, & G. Lindzey (Eds.), *The handbook of social psychology* (4th ed.). New York: McGraw-Hill.

Levine, T. R. & McCornack, S. A. (1992). Linking love and lies: A formal test of the McCornack and Parks model of deception detection. *Journal of Social & Personal Relationships, 9*, 143-154.

Lippard, P. V. (1988). "Ask me no questions, I'll tell you no lies": Situational exigencies for interpersonal deception. *Western Journal of Speech Communication, 52*, 91-103.

Maxwell, G. M. (1985). Behaviour of lovers: Measuring the closeness of relationships. *Journal of Social & Personal Relationships, 2*, 215-238.

McCornack, S. A. & Levine, T. R. (1990). When lies are uncovered: Emotional and relational outcomes of discovered deception. *Communication Monographs, 57*, 119-138.

McCornack, S. A., & Parks, M. R. (1986). Deception detection and relational development: The other side of trust. In M. L. McLaughlin (Ed.), *Communication Yearbook 9* (pp. 377-389). Beverly Hills, Ca: Sage.

Metts, S. (1989). An exploratory investigation of deception in close relationships. *Journal of Social & Personal Relationships, 6*, 159-179.

Millar, K. U. & Tesser, A. (1988). Deceptive behavior in social relationships: A consequence of violated expectations. *Journal of Psychology, 122*, 263-273.

Millar, M. & Millar, K. (1995). Detection of deception in familiar and unfamiliar persons: The effects of information restriction. *Journal of Nonverbal Behavior, 19*, 69-84.

Miller, G. R., Mongeau, P. A. & Sleight, C. (1986). Fudging with friends and lying with lovers: Deceptive communication in personal relationships. *Journal of Social & Personal Relationships, 3*, 495-512.

Nezlek, J. B. (1995). Social construction, gender/sex similarity and social interaction in close personal relationships. *Journal of Social & Personal Relationships, 12*, 503-520.

Parks, M. R. (1982). Ideology in interpersonal communication: Off the couch and into the world. In M. Burgoon (Ed.), *Communication Yearbook 5* (pp. 79-107). New Brunswick, NJ: Transaction Books.

Parks, M. R. & Floyd, K. (1996). Meanings for closeness and intimacy in friendship. *Journal of Social & Personal Relationships, 13*, 85-107.

Reis, H. T., Lin, Y. C., Bennett, E. & Nezlek, J. B. (1993). Change and consistency in social participation during early adulthood. *Developmental Psychology, 29*, 633-645.

Reis, H. T., & Patrick, B. C. (1996). Attachment and intimacy: Component processes. In E. T. Higgins & A. W. Kruglanski (Eds.), *Social psychology: Handbook of basic principles* (pp. 523-563). New York: Guilford Press.

Reis, H. T. & Wheeler, L. (1991). Studying social interaction with the Rochester Interaction Record. *Advances in Experimental Social Psychology,* 24, 269-318.

Ruesch, J., & Bateson, G. (1951). *Communication: The social matrix of psychiatry.* New York: Norton.

Rusbult, C. E., Yovetich, N. A., & Verette, J. (1996). An interdependence analysis of accommodation processes. In G. J. O. Fletcher & J. Fitness (Eds.), *Knowledge structures in close relationships: A social psychological approach* (pp. 63-90). Mahwah, NJ: Erlbaum.

Tice, D. M., Butler, J. L., Muraven, M. B. & Stillwell, A. M. (1995). When modesty prevails: Differential favorability of self-presentations to friends and strangers. *Journal of Personality & Social Psychology,* 69, 1120-1138.

Turner, R. E., Edgley, C. & Olmstead, G. (1975). Informational control in conversations: Honesty is not always the best policy. *Kansas Journal of Sociology,* 11, 69-89.

Watzlawick, P., Beavin, J. H., & Jackson, D. D. (1967). *Pragmatics of human communication: A study of interactional patterns, pathologies, and paradoxes.* New York: Norton.

Wheeler, L. & Nezlek, J. B. (1977). Sex differences in social participation. *Journal of Personality & Social Psychology,* 35, 742-754.

Footnotes

1. The college students in the Metts (1989) study included adult reentry students, but they constituted less than a third of the sample and their data were not analyzed separately.

2. Results from the other measures can be obtained from the authors.

3. Other studies in the literature have also reported descriptive data about relationship characteristics. For example, the mean number of social interactions per day reported by our college students, 6.6, is very similar to the number reported by Reis and Wheeler (1991) for Americans, 6.9. Our community members reported an average of 5.8 social interactions per day. Similarly, in a longitudinal study, Reis and his colleagues noted that participants reported more social interactions per day as college students, 6.9, than they did nearly a decade later, 5.1 (Reis, Lin, Bennett, & Nezlek, 1993). With regard to the correlations among different relationship qualities, our correlations between duration and closeness were stronger than those reported by Berscheid et al. (1989b) and Aron et al. (1991). In the studies reported in the latter article, the correlation between duration and closeness was stronger for men than for women; for women, the correlations were sometimes slightly negative. In our data, the average correlations (computed separately for each participant, omitting family members, and then averaged across participants) were very similar for men and women in the college sample (mean r = .48, n = 30, and mean r = .44, n = 47, respectively). For the community sample, there was a trend in the direction reported by Aron et al. (1992): The correlation was somewhat stronger for the men (mean r = .55, n = 30) than for the women (mean r = .39, n = 39), t (67) = 1.88, p = .06, for the test of the difference between the correlations.

81

4. The results shown in Table 3 were all based on dependent variables that were ratios (i.e., number of lies divided by number of social interactions; number of self-centered or other-oriented lies divided by total number of lies). We also computed alternative analyses that did not involve ratios as dependent measures. To predict rate of lying from closeness and duration, we added number of social interactions as a predictor variable and used number of lies as the dependent variable. To predict self-centered and other-oriented lying from closeness and duration, we added the total number of lies as a predictor variable, and used the number of self-centered or other-oriented lies as the dependent variable. In these analyses, only one effect that was significant using a ratio dependent variable (the effect of duration on overall rate of lying for the community sample) was not even marginally significant in the new analyses (b = −.021). All other patterns remained the same.

5. The n s decrease dramatically in the analyses of self-centered and other-oriented lying, compared with rate of lying. This is because the analyses can include only participants who told lies in at least two dyadic interactions and who told self-centered (or other-oriented) lies in some dyadic interactions and non-self-centered (or non-other-oriented) lies in other dyadic interactions.

Personality and Social Psychology Bulletin, 2002, *28*, 536-545.

The Development of Deception Detection Skill:
A Longitudinal Study of Same-Sex Friends

D. Eric Anderson
Bella M. DePaulo
Matthew E. Ansfield

One member of each of 52 pairs of friends told true and fabricated stories to a partner (the judge) who guessed whether each story was true. The procedure was followed when the friends had known each other for 1 month and again 5 months later. Across all of the pairs, accuracy at detecting deception did not improve over time. However, judges from the emotionally closer pairs did become more accurate at 6 months than they had been at 1 month. The judges from the less-close pairs instead became less inclined to regard the stories as truthful, especially when they actually were truthful. Results of a second study ruled out the alternative interpretation that the closer friends told stories that were more obviously truthful or deceptive at 6 months than they had at 1 month. On indirect measures of deception detection, all of the groups of judges could distinguish the truths from the lies.

People who do not know each other are not very successful at detecting each other's deceptions. Most often, in studies of deception detection skill, people are shown equal numbers of truths and lies and lie detection accuracy is defined as the percentage of both truths and lies that were accurately identified. There are now more than 100 estimates of the lie detection accuracy of people who do not know the person whose truths and lies they are trying to identify and who have no special training or experience at detecting deceit. In these studies, the mean accuracy achieved by the thousands of judges who participated in the studies was 54%. Two thirds of the group accuracy means were between 50% and 59%, and no groups scored higher than the mid-70th percentile. (DePaulo, Tornqvist, & Cooper, 2002).

One important reason for the low levels of accuracy at detecting deception may be that behavioral cues separate truths from lies only probabilistically and usually weakly (DePaulo, Lindsay, et al., 2002). Moreover, there may be important individual differences in cues to deception such that particular behaviors that separate truths from lies for many individuals may not do so for all, and conversely, particular individuals may behave in idiosyncratic ways when lying (cf. Zuckerman, Koestner, & Alton, 1984). If this is so, then a particular person's deception may be most successfully detected by people who have practice and experience at interpreting that person's behavior, such as the person's relationship partners. Over the course of a close personal relationship, people may come to learn the particular behaviors that betray each other's lies and underscore their truths. In addition, their understanding of each other may grow in ways that help them recognize the plausibility or implausibility of the stories they hear within the context of what they know about each other's lives.

In the early phases of a relationship, even relationship partners are unlikely to achieve high levels of accuracy at detecting each other's truths and lies. At first, partners, similar to strangers, have little more than general notions about cues to deception (often erroneous) on which to depend. It could take some time to learn the lie-telling code of another individual. Even over time, however, levels of accuracy will be constrained by inaccurate, delayed, and unsystematic feedback (cf. DePaulo & Pfeifer, 1986; Zuckerman et al., 1984). Subtle cues to deception will be difficult to learn when some lies are never recognized as such, and some unwarranted suspicions are never dispelled (DePaulo, Ansfield, Kirkendol, & Boden, 2002).

There are only a few studies of the deception detection success of groups differing in relationship status, but the results are in line with our dim prognosis. Whether the groups were friends or strangers (Fleming, Darley, Hilton, & Kojetin, 1990), romantic partners and strangers (Anderson, 1999), spouses and friends (Comadena, 1982), or mixed groups of friends and relatives who were compared to strangers (Fleming & Darley, 1991; Millar & Millar, 1995), there were never any unequivocal indications that people in closer relationships would be more successful than those in less-close relationships at detecting each other's deceptions and truths. A few other studies reported correlations between relationship closeness and success at detecting deception within groups of relationship partners, including dating couples (Levine & McCornack, 1992; McCornack & Parks, 1986) and friends (Stiff, Kim, & Ramesh, 1992). All of these correlations were near zero.

The development of a relationship brings not just opportunities to learn a partner's life stories and verbal and nonverbal styles but also emotional needs and investments. One of the most important of these may be people's desire to believe in the honesty of their partners. To sustain that belief, relationship partners may be more likely to show a preference for interpreting each other's communications as truthful than any special insight about deceptiveness. There is some evidence for this preference (typically called a "truth bias" in the deception literature). In the handful of studies comparing groups differing in relationship status, the relationship partners (relatives, friends, and romantic partners) showed an even greater inclination to judge messages as truthful than did strangers (Anderson, 1999; Buller, Strzyzewski, & Hunsaker, 1991; Millar & Millar, 1995). However, there were no indications that within groups of relationship partners (such as dating couples and friends), closeness and the tendency to judge communications as truthful are related (Levine & McCornack, 1992; McCornack & Parks, 1986; Stiff et al., 1992).

Relationship partners' faith in each other may be shaken during the first months of a relationship, as the initial glow of the early weeks gives way to tension and conflict later on (e.g., Hays, 1985). How will relationship partners then interpret each other's behavioral cues to deception and truth? We think that relationship partners who do not feel especially close to each other may no longer show the same generous interpretation of most communications as truthful that they may have shown at the outset. In fact, they may even become more grudging in their readings of each other and disbelieve some communications from their partner that are actually truthful. We predict that only those partners who remain close to each other in the face of the challenges that relationships face over time will show the even-handedness that skillful lie detection demands; that is, they will be secure enough to acknowledge that some of the stories their partner is telling them are lies and trusting enough to recognize the sincerity of the stories that really are truthful (cf. Holmes & Rempel, 1989). In sum, we are predicting that accuracy at detecting deceit will not improve over time for all relationship partners but only for those whose relationships are especially close. In relationships that are less close, we think that the tendency to perceive most communications as truthful will wane.

Our prediction that accuracy at detecting deception will improve over time for people in especially close relationships may seem at odds with the previous studies showing no link between relationship closeness and lie detection success. In some of those studies, the deception detection success of relationship partners was compared to that of strangers. But our prediction is not that relationships partners will outperform strangers, even at detecting the deceit of their own partners, nor is it that people in especially close relationships will do especially well at detecting deception. Instead, it is that especially close relationship partners will become more accurate over time at knowing when their partner is lying or telling the truth. That is a hypothesis that can only be tested longitudinally.

It is possible, however, that even our longitudinal study will uncover no evidence for the development of deception detection skill over the early months of a close personal relationship. But even if relationship partners showed no special detection ability when asked to categorize communications as either truths or lies, we thought we might find evidence for such ability by asking less direct questions. For example, we thought that if we asked participants how comfortable they felt during the interaction, they might report feeling more comfortable when the stories their partner was telling actually were truths than when they were lies. As DePaulo (1994) has suggested, this could occur even if the partners cannot successfully detect deception by their direct categorizations of the stories as truths or lies.

Although the first 100 or so studies in the deception detection literature focused on direct measures, there is now some evidence for indirect deception detection as well. One example comes from an incidental finding from a meta-analysis designed to assess the relationship between confidence and accuracy in the detection of deception (DePaulo, Charlton, Cooper, Lindsay, & Muhlenbruck, 1997). The primary analysis showed that the average correlation between confidence in one's judgments and the accuracy of those judgments was almost exactly zero. However, when the link between judges' self-reports of confidence and the actual truthfulness of the messages was examined, a different story emerged. Judges were more confident when the message they had just rated was a truth than when it was a lie. The judges' reports of differing levels of confidence in their ratings of the truths versus the lies showed that at some level, the judges could differentiate between truths and lies, even though their explicit deception detection accuracy in the same studies was sometimes poor (see also Anderson, DePaulo, Ansfield, Tickle, & Green, 1999).

In the present research, we examine indirect deception detection by relationship partners. We want to know whether friends might be able to detect each other's deception indirectly even when they appear not to have detected it directly (cf. Anderson, 1999). We also want to know whether indirect deception detection increases over time and at different rates than explicit deception detection.

We recruited pairs of men and pairs of women who had known each other for a month and who considered themselves friends. One member of each par, the sender, told four life stories to their friend, the judge, who tried to determine whether the stories were true or fabricated. The judge also completed a series of indirect measures, such as ratings of confidence, comfort, and suspiciousness. Five months later, all but one of the pairs of friends returned and completed the same procedure.

STUDY 1

Method

PARTICIPANTS

Experimenters contacted students from an introductory psychology class at the University of Virginia and asked them to sign up for a study on nonverbal behavior and friendship with a same-sex friend whom they had not known prior to the beginning of the semester. Those who turned in applications and met the criteria specified by the experimenters (including not knowing each other prior to the beginning of the semester and identifying each other as a friend) were contacted and scheduled for the first session of the study. They were then contacted again for a second session, approximately 5 months later. A total of 52 same-sex pairs (29 women, 23 men) completed both sessions.

At the beginning of each of the two sessions, senders and judges completed scales measuring their closeness to each other. The Subjective Closeness Index (see Aaron, Aaron, & Smollan, 1992) was the mean of participants' answers to two questions: "Relative to all your other relationships, how would you characterize your relationship with this person?" and "Relative to what you know about other people's close relationships, how would you characterize your relationship to this person?" Both were answered on scales ranging from 1 (*much less close than others*) to 9 (*much closer than others*). If the mean of the scores for both friends was greater than or equal to 6 at both sessions, the friends were considered especially close. We could have simply used the mean closeness ratings across both time periods; however, by that criterion, a pair of friends with a very high closeness rating at Time 1 but a much lower one at Time 2 (e.g., 7.75 and 5.00 for one of our pairs) would be classified as very close, even though their closeness to each other at Time 2 was only at the midpoint of the scale. We also could have used a simple change criterion to classify our groups, such that the pairs who showed the greatest increase in closeness from Time 1 to Time 2 would be considered the closer friends. However, by that criterion, friends showing a relatively big increase in closeness (e.g., 3.75 and 5.00 for one of our pairs) would be classified as close even thought their closeness was fairly low at both time periods.

According to the criterion we did choose, there were 24 especially close pairs of friends and 28 pairs of friends who were not especially close. The mean closeness ratings of the especially close friends were 6.84 and 7.02 at 1 month and 6 months; for the less-close friends, they were 5.46 and 4.50.

At both sessions, senders and judges also reported their levels of disclosure to each other by indicating whether they had discussed each of 18 topics (Ansfield, DePaulo, & Bell, 1995; Brauer & DePaulo, 1980). Mean scores (averaged across the sender and judge) could therefore range from 0 to 18. A Sex of Dyad X Closeness of Dyad X Time mixed-design ANOVA, with repeated measures on the Time factor, indicated that the closer friends disclosed more to each other than the less-close friends, $Ms = 10.81$ and 7.59, respectively; for the main effect of Closeness, $F(1, 48) = 22.70$, $p < .0001$. This difference did not change significantly over time; for the Closeness X Time interaction, $F(1, 48) = 2.29$, $p = 1.37$.[1]

PROCEDURE

Each pair of friends was tested individually. The friends completed a variety of communication tasks and self-report measures. Only the ones directly relevant to the present report will be described.

In the key task, the friends discussed in turn each of four life stories. One of the friends was randomly assigned to be the sender, who told the stories, and the other was assigned to be the judge, who asked questions about the stories and then tried to determine whether they were true stories. Before each conversation commenced, the judge was given typed instructions that indicated the topic of the story to be discussed (e.g., a story about a relationship; a family story; a story about something that someone once did for, or to, the sender). Story topics were randomly assigned. The judge was instructed to ask the sender to tell a story about that topic. The typed instructions also included hints the judge could use to help the sender think of a relevant story and suggestions for questions the judge could ask to keep the conversation going. The judge's task was to determine, over the course of the conversation, whether the sender was telling a true story. Judges were told that the sender might tell all true stories, all made-up stories, or any combination of true and made-up stories during each session.

Meanwhile, the sender was instructed to tell either a true story or to make up a story (randomly assigned) in response to the judge's questions. The sender could choose any life event that fit the assigned topic as long as it was a story that had never been discussed with the judge. The sender was instructed to make all stories convincing, such that anyone hearing the stories would believe that they were true. Within each session, each sender was instructed to tell two true stories and two fabricated stories. All senders were able to complete this task without difficulty.

After the judge had read the instructions and was ready to begin, the judge and sender sat face-to-face as they discussed the story. They could take up to 4 minutes for each conversation. After each conversation, the sender and judge faced away from each other while they answered a brief questionnaire about the conversation. The judges indicated whether they thought the story was a truth or a lie. They also reported, on 9-point scales, their confidence, comfort, and suspiciousness; the degree to which they tried to hide their suspiciousness; the degree to which they got enough information to make a veracity judgment; their perceptions of their friend's comfort; and their friend's perception of the judge's own suspiciousness. The friends who had told the stories reported whether the story that they had just told was a truth or a lie, as a manipulation check. All storytellers followed the instructions and told the appropriate true or made-up story according to the instructions given by the experimenter.

The same procedure was followed for each of the sessions. The senders and judges maintained their roles across the two sessions.

Table 1

Changes Over Time in Accuracy and Judgments of Truthfulness for the Less-Close Friends and Closer Friends

	Time 1	Time 2	Change
Percentage accuracy			
Less close	56.5	51.2	-5.3
Closer	46.8	61.4	14.6
Percentage judged as true			
Less close	73.9	56.9	-17.0
Closer	61.4	60.4	-1.0

Results

ACCURACY

Sex of dyad, closeness of dyad, and time (1 month, 6 months) were the factors in a mixed-design ANOVA. Time was a repeated-measures factor. Judges' perceptions of the stories as either truths or lies were the dependent measures. Judges were assigned a score of 0 if their perception was incorrect and 1 if it was correct (see Rosenthal & Rosnow, 1991; Snedecor & Cochran, 1967; Winer, 1971, for the use of ANOVA with dichotomous dependent variables). Means can therefore be interpreted straightforwardly as percentage accuracy scores.

The mean accuracy score across all factors in the design was 54.6%. This score, although greater than the chance value of 50%, was not significantly greater, $t(51) = 1.86$, $p = .068$. It is similar to the weighted mean score of 54% across more than 100 studies of lie detection among adults with no special relationship with each other (DePaulo, Tornqvist, & Cooper, 2002). We found no evidence that the judges were better at detecting deception in the closer friendship pairs ($M =$

54.1%) than in the less-close pairs ($M = 53.8\%$), $F(1, 48) < 1$. Also, across all of the pairs of friends, accuracy did not improve significantly from 1 month (51.6%) to 6 months (56.3%); for the main effect of Time, $F(1, 48) = 1.04, p = .313$.

As predicted, closer friends did become more accurate at detecting deception over the course of their relationship (see Table 1); for the Closeness X Time interaction, $F(1, 48) = 4.77, p = .034$. From Time 1 to Time 2, closer friends improved from 46.8% correct to 61.4%, $F(1, 48) = 5.94, p = .019$. For less-close friends, there was a nonsignificant decrease in accuracy from 56.5% to 51.2%, $F = .78, p = .381$. The difference in accuracy between the closer and the less-close friends was not significant at either point in time. For Time 1, $F(1, 48) = 2.66, p = .109$; for Time 2, $F(1, 48) = 2.41, p = .127$.[2]

Table 2

Changes Over Time in Percentage of Truths and lies Judged as Truths by the Closer and the Less-Close Friends

	Less-Close Friends			Closer Friends		
	Time 1	Time 2	Change	Time 1	Time 2	Change
Truths	80.4	58.1	-22.3	58.2	71.8	13.6
Lies	67.4	55.8	-11.6	64.6	48.9	-15.7

PERCENTAGE OF STORIES JUDGED AS TRUE

Sex and closeness were again between-dyad factors, and time and truthfulness of the story (truth, lie) were repeated-measures factors in an ANOVA with truth judgments as the dependent variable. Judges were assigned a score of 0 if they judged the story to be a lie and 1 if they judged it to be a truth. Means therefore indicate the percentage of messages judged to be truths.

Even though only half of the stories they heard really were truths, judges believed that 63.7% of them were truths. Therefore, as in many previous studies (DePaulo, Tornqvist, & Cooper, 2002; Levine, McCornack, & Park, 1999), judges showed a tendency to judge significantly more than half of the messages as truths, $t(51) = 5.58, p < .0001$. This tendency decreased from 1 month (67.7%) to 6 months (58.6%); for the main effect of Time, $F(1, 48) = 5.43, p = .024$.

There was no difference between the closer friends (60.9%) and the less-close friends (65.4%) in their overall tendency to judge the stories as truthful; for the main effect of Closeness, $F(1, 48) = .82, p = .371$. However, the decrease over time in the tendency to judge stories as truthful was specific to the less-close friends; for the Closeness X Time interaction, $F(1, 48) = 4.22, p = .046$. As shown in Table 1, the less-close friends believed that 73.9% of the stories were true at Time 1 but only 56.9% at Time 2. In contrast, the closer friends consistently judged about 60% of the stories to be true.

The three-way interaction of Closeness, Time, and Truthfulness of the story (statistically identical to the significant two-way interaction of Closeness X Time in the accuracy ANOVA) addresses the question of whether the closer friends' improvement in accuracy resulted from an improvement in identifying truths as truths or in identifying lies as lies, or both. It also indicates whether the less-close friends made any particular error (misidentifying truths as lies or lies as truths) more often at one time than another. As shown in Table 2, the closer friends improved over time both in seeing the truths as truths, $F(1, 48) = 2.31$, $p = .135$, and the lies as lies, $F(1, 48) = 3.08$, $p = .086$, although neither individual comparison was significant. The less-close friends tended to see all of the messages as less truthful at Time 2 than at Time 1, and this drop in truthfulness judgments was significant for the messages that actually were truthful, $F(1, 48) = 6.22$, $p = .016$. (For the lies, $F[1, 48] = 1.68$, $p = .201$.)

INDIRECT MEASURES

To assess indirect deception detection, we asked the judges how confident they were in their guesses, how comfortable they were, how comfortable they thought the senders were, how suspicious they were, how much they tried to hide their suspicion, how suspicious the senders thought they were, and the extent to which they had gotten enough information to make their judgments of truthfulness. The answers to these questions were analyzed in a MANOVA using the same factors as in the ANOVA conducted on the explicit guesses.

As predicted, there was a main multivariate effect for the actual truthfulness of the story, $F(7, 41) = 4.16$, $p = .002$. All seven of the univariate tests were significant or nearly so. The univariate analyses revealed that judges were more confident in their guesses when the story was true ($M = 6.38$) than when it was made up ($M = 5.75$), $F(1, 48) = 10.78$, $p = .0019$, were more comfortable when the story was true ($M = 7.56$) than when it was false ($M = 7.13$), $F(1, 47) = 14.27$, $p = .0004$, were less suspicious during the true stories ($M = 4.88$) than during the made-up ones ($M = 5.51$), $F(1, 48) = 9.13$, $p = .004$, tried to hide suspicion slightly less during the true stories ($M = 3.62$) than during made-up stories ($M = 3.97$), $F(1, 48) = 3.78$, $p = .058$, and felt that they got more information during the true stories ($M = 6.52$) than during the made-up stories ($M = 5.82$), $F(1, 48) = 19.48$, $p = .0001$.

Judges also thought that the senders were more comfortable during the true stories ($M = 6.83$) than during the made-up ones ($M = 6.36$), $F(1, 48) = 7.73$, $p = .008$, and believed the senders perceived them as less suspicious during the true stories ($M = 4.60$) than during the made-up stories ($M = 5.01$), $F(1, 48) = 4.14$, $p = .048$.

There was also a main, multivariate effect for time of measurement, $F(7, 41) = 2.52$, $p = .030$. The significant univariate effects indicated that judges saw the senders as more comfortable at Time 1 ($M = 6.88$) than at Time 2 ($M = 6.31$), $F(1, 48) = 6.67$, $p = .013$, and that the judges tried to hide their suspicion more at Time 1 ($M = 4.21$) than they did at Time 2 ($M = 3.38$), $F(1, 48) = 6.88, p = .012$.

If the closer friends were more accurate than the less-close friends on the indirect measures, the Truthfulness of the Story X Closeness interaction would be significant. If the closer friends, relative to the less-close friends, became more accurate on the indirect measures only over time, then the Truthfulness of Story X Closeness X Time interaction would be significant. However, neither of these effects was significant. (For the two-way interaction, $F[7, 35] = 1.96, p = .089$; for the three-way interaction, $F[7, 41] = 1.64, p = .152$.)[3]

Discussion

It was only the judges from the closer friendship pairs in Study 1 who improved significantly in deception detection accuracy from about 1 month into their friendship until 5 months later. These closer friends did not seem to have selected each other on the basis of their initial ability to detect each other's truths and les because, at Time 1, the closer friends were slightly less accurate than the less-close friends. The closer friends were not even better than the less-close friends in the degree to which they could distinguish the truths from the lies on dimensions other than truthfulness, because indirect accuracy was the same for both groups at both points in time. Instead, our preferred explanation is that only the closer judges learned to interpret cues more accurately over time.

However, there are other possible explanations. For example, the senders from the closer pairs may have told truths and lies that were more clearly recognizable as such at Time 2 than they had at Time 1. If this did in fact occur, then anyone watching the Time 2 tapes of their stories should be able to show the same accuracy at detecting the truths and lies that their friends did. To test this, we recruited raters who were strangers to the original participants to view the videotapes of the friends' interactions and record their impressions.

Study 1 also left unanswered several questions about the interpretation of the indirect deception detection effects. Both the less-close and the closer friends could detect deception on these measures. Does that suggest that even the less-close friends, who were inept at detecting deception directly, did have some special ability to discriminate truths from lies or would even strangers be able to make these distinctions when watching the interactions on videotape? Again, the recruitment of strangers as raters allows us to answer this.

Finally, the indirect deception detection measures were continuous measures, whereas the direct deception detection index was dichotomous. Perhaps it is this measurement difference that accounts for the greater accuracy on indirect than direct measures. To address this, we added a continuous measure of truthfulness.

STUDY 2

Method

PARTICIPANTS

Raters for this study were undergraduate research assistants who received course credit for their work. Eight raters (4 men, 4 women) each rated all 104 of the tapes (52 pairs x 2 sessions).

PROCEDURE

Raters watched the conversations from Study 1 in a counterbalanced order. Half of the raters watched tapes from Time 1 first, whereas the other half watched tapes from Time 2 first. Furthermore, half of the raters in each of those two conditions watched the tapes of the male dyads first, whereas the other half watched the tapes of the female dyads first. Finally, half of the raters in each condition watched the tapes of the particular friendship pairs in the order in which they were originally run and the other half watched the tapes in the reverse order.

The raters filled out many of the same measures as the friends in Study 1, including the question about whether they thought each story was the truth or a lie, and a measure that the friends did not complete, a 9-point rating of the truthfulness of the communication (1 = *not at all truthful*, 9 = *completely truthful*). They also indicated their perceptions of the sender's comfort and the judge's comfort and the judge's suspiciousness. In addition, they rated their own comfort, suspiciousness, and confidence in their judgments and indicated the degree to which they felt that they had gotten enough information to make their judgments.

Results

ANALYSES

Accuracy and truth bias were computed for the Study 2 raters as they were for the Study 1 friends. Friendship pairs were again the units of analysis. Within-pair factors were time (1 month, 6 months); order of judgment (Time 1 tapes first, Time 2 tapes first); sex of rater; and for the ANOVA on judgments that the story was true, truthfulness of the story (truth, lie). Sex of dyad and closeness of the pair were the between-pairs factors. All of those factors were also included in an ANOVA in which the 9-point ratings of truthfulness were the dependent measures. Finally, a MANOVA with the same factors was computed on all of the indirect deception detection measures.

COULD STRANGERS DISTINGUISH TRUTHS FROM LIES?

There were three assessments of whether the raters in Study 2, who were strangers to the people they were judging on the videotapes, could distinguish the truths from the lies: the dichotomous, explicit measure of detection accuracy that was used in Study 1; a set of indirect measures; and a continuous scale of truthfulness. As in Study 1, explicit accuracy based on judgments of the stories as truths or lies was not significantly greater than chance, $M = 50.6\%$, $t(51) = 1.43$, $p = .159$.

To determine whether the raters detected deception indirectly, their answers to questions about their confidence in their guesses, their level of suspicion, their perceptions of the judge's level of suspicion, the extent to which they got enough information to make their veracity judgments, and their perceptions of both the sender's and judge's levels of comfort were entered into a MANOVA. As in Study 1, the indirect measures separated the truths from the lies. There was a significant multivariate main effect for the truthfulness of the story, $F(6, 43) = 42.70$, $p < .0001$. Raters were more confident of their guesses when the story was true ($M = 5.30$) than when it was made up ($M = 5.21$), $F(1, 48) = 12.71$, $p = .0008$, thought that the senders were more comfortable during true stories ($M = 5.90$) than during fabricated stories ($M = 5.78$), $F(1, 48) = 21.17$, $p < .0001$, and thought that the judges were more suspicious during the fabricated stories ($M = 5.05$) than during the true stories ($M = 4.48$), $F(1, 48) = 307.0$, $p < .0001$. Raters were also more suspicious when viewing clips of the lies ($M = 4.81$) than when they saw clips of the truths ($M = 4.26$), $F(1, 48) = 96.1$, $p < .0001$. Raters also reported that they got more information on which to base their judgment of truthfulness when they heard a true story ($M = 5.10$) than when they heard a fabricated one ($M = 5.03$), $F(1, 48) = 7.37$, $p = .009$.

The third index of detection ability, the continuous measure of truthfulness, was new to this study. The main effect of the truthfulness of the story was significant for this measure, $F(1, 48) = 8.92$, $p = .004$, and showed that accuracy on this measure was greater than chance: Raters judged the stories that were actually true to be more truthful ($M = 5.10$) than the stories that were actually made up ($M = 4.98$).

DID THE DECEPTION OF THE CLOSER FRIENDS BECOME MORE OBVIOUS OVER TIME?

In Study 1, the judges from the closer pairs showed significant improvement over time at detecting their friend's deception. If this result occurred because the senders in the closer dyads told lies that were more easily distinguished from truths at 6 months than at 1 month, then the lies should be especially distinguishable from the truths even to strangers. This would be evident in a Closeness X Time of Measurement effect for raters' accuracy. This effect was not significant, $F(1, 48) = 2.49$, $p = .121$. (The direction of the effect indicated that the raters were less accurate at judging both the closer and the less-close friends from the Time 2 tapes, $Ms = 50.4$ and 47.5, respectively, than from the Time 1 tapes, $M = 52.5$ for both groups.)

Were there any indications that the lies told by the closer friends became more detectable over time on the indirect measures of detection or on the continuous truthfulness scale? Such effects would result in a three-way interaction of Closeness, Time of Measurement, and Truthfulness of

93

the Story. This interaction was not significant in the multivariate analysis, $F(6, 43) = .75$, $p = .614$, or in the truthfulness ANOVA, $F(1, 48) = .59$, $p = .445$.

GENERAL DISCUSSION

The Development of Deception Detection Skill: Relationship Closeness

The present study is the first to trace deception detection accuracy over the development of a friendship, from the first month to 6 months into the relationship. Overall, the friends in our first study were as successful at detecting deception as strangers. Their accuracy was slightly, but not significantly, above chance, and they guessed that more of the stories were true than made up, despite hearing equal numbers of each. As a group, the judges showed only an insignificant degree of improvement at detecting the deception of their friends from the time when they had known them only for about a month until 5 months later. In fact, the overall accuracy of the friends across both time periods, 54.6%, was very similar to the 54% accuracy for strangers, documented across more than 100 estimates (DePaulo, Tornqvist, & Cooper, 2002). If we had examined only our group of friends as a whole, we would have come to the same conclusion as previous cross-sectional studies, namely, that there is no unqualified evidence that relationship partners are better than strangers at detecting deception (Anderson, Ansfield, & DePaulo, 1999).

In previous research, the link between closeness and accuracy at detecting deception also had been assessed by correlating closeness with accuracy within groups of relationship partners. We computed analogous correlations from our data separately for Time 1 and Time 2. As in the earlier studies, we too found unimpressive results when we treated our data as if they were cross-sectional. The correlation of closeness with accuracy was $r(50) = -.112$ at Time 1 and .102 at Time 2.

We thought that friends who remained especially close after knowing each other for 6 months would show greater accuracy than they had at 1 month. Close friends' ability to maintain and sometimes even deepen their intimacy, we thought, could have been gained by their success at dealing with annoyances, inconveniences, and threats (Holmes & Rempel, 1989). They would thereby have less need than other relationship partners either to believe that their friend would never tell lies or to be overly suspicious of their friend.

As we predicted, the closer friends showed a significant improvement in deception detection accuracy from 1 month to 6 months, whereas the less-close friends showed a trivial decrease in accuracy. We considered the alternative that accuracy improved in the closer friendship pairs not because the judges were becoming more insightful but because their friends who were telling the stories were becoming more obvious. However, our Study 2 data were inconsistent with that alternative. The strangers rating the videotapes were no more successful at detecting the closer friends' truths and deceptions told at Time 2 than those told at Time 1.

94

The failure of the judges in the less-close pairs to show any improvement over time was accounted for by a consistent mistake they made: At 6 months, they often disbelieved their friends, even when their friends deserved to be believed. Whereas at 1 month they believed in the truthfulness of 80.4% of the stories that actually were true, by 6 months, they believed that only 58.1% of the truthful stories were true. The emotionally closer friends instead became increasingly well calibrated in the appropriateness of their faithfulness and skepticism. From 1 month to 6 months, they believed more of their friends' truths and disbelieved more of their lies (although neither of these comparisons, tested individually, was significant).

We have been focusing on the differential interpretation of cues by the closer and less-close friends once those cues have been noticed. It is also possible that the closer friends were more attentive to each other and thereby recognized more of the potentially relevant cues in the first place. We were able to assess the degree to which the judges noticed some differences between truths and lies by our measures of indirect deception detection. Of interest, both the closer and the less-close judges, at both points in time, successfully separated the truths from the lies on these indirect measures; so did the raters from Study 2, who were strangers to the senders. The levels of indirect deception detection were very consistent. They were comparable for the closer and the less-close judges, and they were stable from Time 1 to Time 2. From what we can discern from the results of our indirect measures, then, differential recognition of potentially relevant cues did not account for the development of skill at detecting a partner's deception that was unique to the closer friends.

Given that all of the groups and subgroups showed significant indirect deception detection at both time periods, why is it that only the closer friends at Time 2 performed significantly better than chance on the direct, dichotomous measure of deception detection? The distinctions that perceivers made on the indirect measures, although quite reliable statistically, were not large when considered in terms of points on the rating scales. For example, on the 9-point scale of suspiciousness, judges recorded a mean rating of 5.51 when their friends were telling lies, compared to a mean rating of 4.88 when their friends were telling the truth. To the friends making these judgments, their impressions probably seemed more like hints than compelling evidence. That left lots of room for the judges to interpret their intuitions in the context of their wishes and fears about their relationship partners. For the close friends at Time 2, who had maintained their closeness over the course of the 6 months, despite any conflicts and disappointments that may have arisen, it was possible to take the glimmer of sincerity they heard in the honest stories and believe in their friends' truthfulness. At the same time, the close friends were also willing to accept rather than deny the whiff of insincerity they discerned in the dishonest stories and call those stories lies. For the less-close friends, however, faith in their partners had apparently eroded over time. A mere glimmer of sincerity was not reason enough to give their friends credit for being truthful, whereas a whiff of insincerity was considered more than sufficient justification for calling their friends liars (see also Holmes & Rempel, 1989; Rempel, Holmes, & Zanna, 1985). This explanation is, however, admittedly speculative.

Because our direct measure of deception detection in Study 1 was dichotomous, whereas our indirect measures were continuous, it is possible that judges only seemed to be more accurate on the indirect measures because those were more sensitive measures. To clarify this point, we added a continuous measure of truthfulness, which is a direct assessment of perceptions of truthfulness on a more sensitive scale. The Study 2 raters did show significant deception detection accuracy on the continuous measure, even though they did not perform significantly better than chance on the direct dichotomous measure. This suggests that the dichotomous and indirect measures may differ more importantly on measurement sensitivity than on directness.

However, we are cautious about this conclusion for a number of reasons. First, ratings on several of the indirect measures separated the truths from the lies even more strongly than did the ratings on the truthfulness scale. Second, in several previous studies (e.g., DePaulo, Jordan, Irvine, & Laser, 1992; DePaulo, Rosenthal, Green, & Rosenkrantz, 1982), both the direct and the indirect perceptions were assessed on the same type of rating scale but accuracy was greater on the indirect measures. The only study other than the present ones designed specifically to address direct and indirect deception detection was Anderson's (1999) investigation of the detection of deception by romantic partners and strangers. In that study, judges were given the potentially threatening task of assessing the truthfulness of people (sometimes their romantic partners) who were answering the question of whether they found a specific other person attractive. On the direct dichotomous measure, perceivers were significantly less accurate when the person they were judging was a romantic partner than when that person was a stranger (cf. Simpson, Ickes, & Blackstone, 1995). On the indirect, continuous measures, however, judgments of the romantic partners were significantly more accurate. The results for the rating scale measures of truthfulness, which was a direct but sensitive measure, were the same as for the direct dichotomous measure: When judges had to make direct ratings of deceptiveness, they were less insightful about their own romantic partners than they were about total strangers. The Anderson (1999) findings, together with our own, point to the importance of continuing the study of direct and indirect deception detection in different relationship types and with deception tasks varying in the potential threat they pose to the relationship.

Other Alternatives and Qualifications

We have argued that close friends' improved success at detecting deception followed from their increasingly accurate interpretation of specific behavioral cues. Alternatively, the judges from the closer pairs may have become more accurate because they had come to know their friends more deeply and therefore could interpret the plausibility of their stories more knowledgeably (cf. Stinson & Ickes, 1992). Within the context of an especially intimate relationship, the same stories that might seem convincing to a stranger could be more transparently false to a friend. We know that in the present research, the friends in the closer pairs, relative to those from the less-close pairs, did disclose more to each other. However, when we included the mean disclosure scores from the friendship pairs at each point in time as covariates, the previously significant Sex X Time effect, $F(1, 48) = 4.77$, $p = .034$, dropped only slightly to $F(1, 47) = 3.27$, $p = .077$.

96

Therefore, we think it is unlikely that this explanation fully accounts for the closer friends' improvement in accuracy.

Another alternative explanation is that at Time 2, the senders from the closer pairs deliberately told truths and lies that would be distinguishable only to their friend and not to strangers (cf. Fleming & Darley, 1991; Fleming et al., 1990). Because the participants followed the experimental procedure in every other way, we think it is unlikely that they chose to subvert it in this one way, but we cannot rule it out.

One limitation of our study is that we tracked our friends for only 6 months. Although there is a deepening and stabilizing of friendships within that time frame (Hays, 1985), it is possible that 6 months marks just the beginning of the development of skills as difficult as detecting deceit. If we followed our friends for a much longer period of time, they may have shown much more impressive gains. Although this possibility may be worth pursuing, we are not very optimistic. The 61.4% accuracy achieved by the closer friends at 6 months is a score bested by fewer than 10% of the groups of strangers recently reviewed meta-analytically (DePaulo, Tornqvist, & Cooper, 2002). Even among professionals whose jobs involve daily attempts to detect lies, accuracy scores greater than the mid-60th percentile are uncommon (e.g., DePaulo & Pfeifer, 1986; Ekman & O'Sullivan, 1991; Ekman, O'Sullivan, & Frank, 1999). Relationship partners, similar to experienced professionals, have many opportunities to learn about cues to deception, but under many circumstances, the behavioral indicators of deception are likely to remain subtle and ambiguous. Whether relationship partners draw the correct inferences from those cues may depend importantly on whether they are willing to own up to the implications of those inferences – for example, that their partner is not so saintly as they had wished or so demonic as they had alleged.

NOTES

1. There was also a main effect for Sex of Dyad, $F(1, 48) = 7.75$, $p = .008$, indicating that the female friends disclosed more to each other ($M = 10.14$) than did the male friends ($M = 8.26$).

2. About ½ hour after judges indicated their guesses as to whether their friends had told the truth or lied about each story, they were asked to record their guesses once again about the same stories. When the two different guesses were added to the analysis as levels of a repeated-measures factor, the Sex of Dyad X Time interaction became significant, $F(1, 50) = 4.49$, $p < .05$. This interaction showed that, averaging across the two guesses, the women's accuracy improved from 48% at Time 1 to 59% at Time 2, whereas the men's accuracy decreased slightly from 52% to 48%. The interaction of Sex and Time with the particular guess was not significant, suggesting that the pattern of means was essentially the same for the two guesses. However, the Sex X Time interaction was not significant in the analysis reported in this article, $F(1, 48) = 1.62$, $p = .210$, which was conducted on just the first guesses.

3. Because this effect was important to our interpretation, we checked the results of the univariate analyses. The effect was not significant in any of those analyses either.

Authors' Note: The studies were supported in part by grants from the National Science Foundation and the National Institute of Mental Health to the second author. We thank Reginald B. Adams for his help with this research.

REFERENCES

Anderson, D. E. (1999). *Cognitive and motivational processes underlying the truth bias*. Unpublished doctoral dissertation, University of Virginia.

Anderson, D. E., Ansfield, M. E., & DePaulo, B. M. (1999). Love's best habit: Deception in the context of relationships. In P. Philippot, R. S. Feldman, & E. J. Coats (Eds.), *The social context of nonverbal behavior* (pp. 372-409). Cambridge, UK: Cambridge University Press.

Anderson, D. E., DePaulo, B. M., Ansfield, M. E., Tickle, J. J., & Green, E. (1999). Beliefs about cues to deception: Mindless stereotypes or untapped wisdom? *Journal of Nonverbal Behavior, 23,* 67-88.

Ansfield, M. E., DePaulo, B. M., & Bell, K. L. (1995). Familiarity effects in nonverbal understanding: Recognizing our own facial expressions and our friends'. *Journal of Nonverbal Behavior, 19,* 135-149.

Aron, A., Aron, E. A., & Smollan, D. (1992). Inclusion of the Other in the Self Scale and the structure of interpersonal closeness. *Journal of Personality and Social Psychology, 63,* 592-612.

Brauer, D. V., & DePaulo, B. M. (1980). Similarities between friends in their understanding of nonverbal cues. *Journal of Nonverbal Behavior, 5,* 64-68.

Buller, D. B., Strzyzewski, K. D., & Hunsaker, F. G. (1991). Interpersonal deception: II. The inferiority of conversational participants as deception detectors. *Communication Monographs, 58,* 25-40.

Comadena, M. E. (1982). Accuracy in detecting deception: Intimate and friendship relationships. In M. Burgoon & N. E. Doran (Eds.), *Communication yearbook 6* (pp. 446-472). Beverly Hills, CA: Sage.

DePaulo, B. M. (1994). Spotting lies: Can humans learn to do better? *Current Directions in Psychological Science, 3,* 83-86.

DePaulo, B. M., Ansfield, M. E., Kirkendol, S. E., & Boden, J. M. (2002). *Serious lies*. Manuscript submitted for review.

DePaulo, B. M., Charlton, K., Cooper, H., Lindsay, J. J., & Muhlenbruck, L. (1997). The accuracy-confidence correlation in the detection of deception. *Personality and Social Psychology Review, 1,* 346-357.

DePaulo, B. M., Jordan, A., Irvine, A., & Laser, P. S. (1982). Age changes in the detection of deception. *Child Development, 53,* 701-709.

DePaulo, B. M., Lindsay, J. J., Malone, B. E., Muhlenbruck, L., Charlton, K., & Cooper, H. (2002). *Cues to deception*. Manuscript submitted for review.

DePaulo, B. M., & Pfeifer, R. L. (1986). On-the-job experience and skill at detecting deception. *Journal of Applied Social Psychology*, *16*, 249-267.

DePaulo, B. M., Rosenthal, R., Green, C. R., & Rosenkrantz, J. (1982). Diagnosing deceptive and mixed messages from verbal and nonverbal cues. *Journal of Experimental Social Psychology*, *18*, 433-446.

DePaulo, B. M., Tornqvist, J. S., & Cooper, H. (2002). *Accuracy at detecting deception: A meta-analysis of modality effects*. Manuscript in preparation.

Ekman, P., & O'Sullivan, M. (1991). Who can catch a liar? *American Psychologist*, *46*, 913-920.

Ekman, P., O'Sullivan, M., & Frank, M. G. (1999). A few can catch a liar. *Psychological Science*, *10*, 263-266.

Fleming, J. H., & Darley, J. M. (1991). Mixed messages: The multiple audience problem and strategic communication. *Social Cognition*, *9*, 29-46.

Fleming, J. H., Darley, J. M., Hilton, J. L., & Kojetin, B. A. (1990). Multiple audience problem: A strategic communication perspective on social perception. *Journal of Personality and Social Psychology*, *58*, 593-609.

Hays, R. B. (1985). A longitudinal study of friendship development. *Journal of Personality and Social Psychology*, *48*, 909-924.

Holmes, J. G., & Rempel, J. K. (1989). Trust in close relationships. In C. Hendrick (Ed.), *Review of personality and social psychology: Close relationships* (Vol. 10, pp. 187-220). Newbury Park, CA: Sage.

Levine, T. R., & McCornack, S. A. (1992). Linking love and lies: A formal test of the McCornack and Parks model of deception detection. *Journal of Social and Personal Relationships*, *9*, 143-154.

Levine, T. R., McCornack, S. A., & Park, H. S. (1999). Accuracy in detecting truth and lies: Documenting the "veracity effect." *Communication Monographs*.

McCornack, S. A., & Parks, M. R. (1986). Deception detection and relationship development: The other side of trust. In M. L. McLaughlin (Ed.), *Communication yearbook 9*. Beverly Hills, CA: Sage.

Millar, M., & Millar, K. (1995). Detection of deception in familiar and unfamiliar persons: The effects of information restriction. *Journal of Nonverbal Behavior*, *19*, 69-84.

Rempel, J. K., Holmes, J. G., & Zanna, M. P. (1985). Trust in close relationships. *Journal of Personality and Social Psychology*, *49*, 95-112.

Rosenthal, R., & Rosnow, R. L. (1991). *Essentials of behavioral research* (2nd ed.). New York: McGraw Hill.

Simpson, J. A., Ickes, W., & Blackstone, T. (1995). When the head protects the heart: Empathic accuracy in dating relationships. *Journal of Personality and Social Psychology*, *69*, 629-641.

Snedecor, J. C., & Cochran, W. G. (1967). *Statistical methods* (6th ed.). Ames: Iowa State University Press.

Stiff, J. B., Kim, H. J., & Ramesh, C. N. (1992). Truth biases and aroused suspicion in relational deception. *Communication Research*, *19*, 326-345.

Stinson, L., & Ickes, W. (1992). Empathic accuracy in the interactions of male friends versus male strangers. *Journal of Personality and Social Psychology*, *62*, 787-797.

Winer, B. J. (1971). *Statistical principles in experimental design* (3rd ed.). New York: McGraw-Hill.

Zuckerman, M., Koestner, R., & Alton, A. O. (1984). Learning to detect deception. *Journal of Personality and Social Psychology*, *46*, 519-528.

About the Author

Bella DePaulo (PhD, Harvard) has authored more than 100 scholarly publications. Her expertise on topics such as friendship, singlehood, and the psychology of deception has been recognized in the *New York Times*, the *Washington Post*, *USA Today*, the *Wall Street Journal*, and many other major national and international newspapers. Her work has also been reported in magazines such as *Time*, *Newsweek*, *The Week*, *AAR P Magazine*, *Business Week*, *More*, the *New York Times Magazine*, and the *New Yorker*. Her op-ed essays have appeared in publications such as the *New York Times*, the *Chronicle of Higher Education*, and *Forbes*. Dr. DePaulo has discussed her work on ABC, NBC, CBS, CNN, CNBC, PBS, the BBC, and the Discovery Channel. She has lectured nationally and internationally, addressing such diverse groups as medical professionals, forensic scientists, school teachers, criminal attorneys, physicists, judges, women's centers, and mental health practitioners.

She writes the "Living Single" blog for *Psychology Today*, and is also a contributor to the Huffington Post. She has been a Visiting Professor of Psychology at the University of California, Santa Barbara since the summer of 2000. Much more information about her background, her books, and her contact information, together with her *All Things Single (and More)* blog, can be found at her website, www.BellaDePaulo.com.

Other Books by Bella DePaulo

Singled Out:
How Singles Are Stereotyped, Stigmatized, and Ignored, and Still Live Happily Ever After

Single with Attitude:
Not Your Typical Take on Health and Happiness, Love and Money, Marriage and Friendship

The Psychology of Dexter

The Lies We Tell and the Clues We Miss:
Professional Papers

Behind the Door of Deceit:
Understanding the Biggest Liars in Our Lives

The Hows and Whys of Lies